Monkery Bottom

BY

John J. S. Roders

Order this book online at www.trafford.com
or email orders@trafford.com

Most Trafford titles are also available at major online book retailers.

Printed in Victoria, BC, Canada.

ISBN: 978-1-4269-2146-9 (sc)

ISBN: 978-1-4269-2147-6 (dj)

Library of Congress Control Number: 2009912489

*Our mission is to efficiently provide the world's finest, most comprehensive book publishing
service, enabling every author to experience success. To find out how to publish your book, your
way, and have it available worldwide, visit us online at www.trafford.com*

Trafford rev. 12/03/2009

 www.trafford.com

North America & international
toll-free: 1 888 232 4444 (USA & Canada)
phone: 250 383 6864 ◆ fax: 812 355 4082

Preface

Adelaide was from a large middle class family with Jewish roots, living in the more affluent West End of London. Tim was an Irish immigrant, escaping the poverty of his homeland and living along the docks in the East End with the labouring poor. This area was a slum, alive with all manner of vermin. The streets were fouled with horse dung and urine. Here, Tim did battle each day for what little work there might be available on the docks.

How Tim and Adelaide ever met was a mystery that has always puzzled the family. Threatened with expulsion from the family by her mother and father, Adelaide went ahead and married Tim. What followed was a lifetime of mistreatment. Apart from Tim's violent ways, and the poverty of living in the East End, there was the birth of eight children that took its toll on Adelaide's body, both mentally and physically. Growing up in this chaotic family, deprived of many of the basic needs of life, Tilly watched her mother struggle to keep house, home and marriage together, and food on the table for her eight children.

The story follows a period of Tilly's life from the time

her farther first marched off to fight in WW1, until she immigrated to Canada with her own two children in 1961. The account parallels the struggles of her own mother's life to Tilly's life as she endeavoured to raise two children as a single parent.

Epigraph

A beloved mother who had stood tall in the face of many adversities, and instilled in us the will to work, as if she had foreseen the turbulent future that would lay ahead for one of her brood.

For Tilly

My Mother and friend
She filled our days with happiness.

Karen
Who shared the journey

Ruth
The love of my life

Timothy and Steven
Diamonds in the rough.

Contents

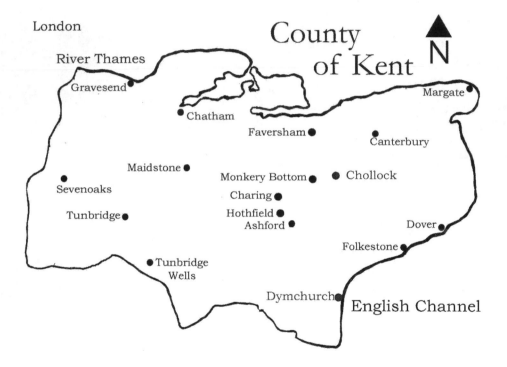

London

River Thames

County
of Kent

N

Gravesend

Margate

Chatham

Faversham

Canterbury

Maidstone

Monkery Bottom

Chollock

Sevenoaks

Charing

Tunbridge

Hothfield

Ashford

Dover

Folkestone

Tunbridge
Wells

Dymchurch

English Channel

Chapter 1

A foggy day in London

As your days, so shall your strength be

London, Monday December 27ᵗʰ, 1909. It was a bitterly cold winter day, thick grey smog hung low over the city. The sound of foghorns coming from ships on the river had a mournful echo to them. Tim left early that morning for the docks where he hoped to pick up a bit of part time work. Adelaide, with two young daughters and another child on the way, busied herself with some sewing she had taken in to earn a few extra pennies. While pumping away on the pedal of her sewing machine, and waiting for Tim to return home, she began to feel the familiar pains of labour. Knowing though, as the time passed, Tim would not be home anytime soon. Chances were that either he was down at the pub squandering whatever money he had made that day, or, if he had not worked, he would be using his Irish charm to cadge a few shots of whisky. It was now six thirty, and with hungry mouths waiting to eat, she took some pork left over from Christmas, watered it down and made a soup.

At eight thirty with labour pains increasing, Adelaide sent her daughter Rose next door to fetch the neighbour lady, while young Addy ran down to the pub to see if she could find her father. At nine o'clock, in full labour and with no sign of Tim, Adelaide gave birth to her third child, another baby girl. This grey and gloomy night would be an ominous foreboding of the turbulent times that would lay ahead for this third child.

Tim finally arrived home at ten thirty, drunk, disorderly and in a foul mood. Discontent over the circumstances of his life, he took his frustrations out verbally on Mrs. Morgan, the neighbour lady who had stepped in as mid-wife. She in turn berated him for coming home in such a state.

A few days later mother and father took Matilda Maud down to the local registry office to record her birth, with one small error. Father, suffering from the effects of another night out on the booze, spelt the last name "Reagen," a mistake that would come back to trouble Tilly some years later.

Here, in Tilly's own words, are some of the stories she shared with me of her life while she was growing up in London.

One of my earliest recollections of my father while growing up in London was of him marching off to war. I was only five at the time when the "First World War" started. Father had found very little work at the docks this particular day and had spent the afternoon at the pub, talking with an arm forces recruiting officer. Returning home, and feeling no pain, he announced to mother that he had joined the army. Down at the local recruiting center, he had signed on the dotted line, accepted the King's shilling, and would be shipping out very shortly. A few days later, to the strains of "Good-bye Dolly Gray", he marched off to war.

With a shortage of men, women were called on to pick up the slack and for the first time in their lives, became serious wage earners. Willing to do their part, mother and a few of the neighbourhood women picked up their shovels and strode off to the local gas works to shovel coke into the retorts. After all, they were told patriotically, "This was a war to end all wars; England was going to be a land fit for heroes to live in when it was all over." Matching the men shovel for shovel as they fed the giant furnaces, the women took their share of insults from them. One day, fed up with all the bullshit, mother confronted the instigator and said to him, "Why don't you lay down your shovel ya gutless bastard and go pick up a gun," Then with one mighty swing of the shovel, she knocked him head first into a pile of coke, much to the delight of her shovel waving mates. From then on, the men were mindful of the women and treated them with a little more regard.

With money and food in short supply, the women at the gas works hatched a plan to rob a local German Bakery of its bread and flour supply. They came away that night with enough swag to last the three of them for months. Until word went around that the bakery had got wind of their plan and had laced the flour and bread with rat poison. Not wanting to take a chance on eating any of the ill-gotten gains, they late one night took it all down to the Thames and sadly tossed it all in the river.

With very little concept of the perils of the war and in the company of the rest of the kids on the street, we would march right up behind the soldiers as the bands lead them off to war, cheering, waving and giving them the thumbs up. In school, we would watch the zeppelins out of the window as they drifted across the sky. The teacher, bewildered by this class of unrefined learners, would hustle us beneath the school during a raid, much to our delight, having escaped the boredom of the classroom for another day.

At home, there were not a lot of toys to play with. Rope pinched from a neighbour's clothesline and slung around a street lamp made a great swing, or another short piece for a skipping rope. Hopscotch was a popular pastime for the girls, while wickets chalked out on a wall were sufficient for the boys to play a game of cricket. The highlight of the week was the water cart, as it made its way around the dung-slick streets washing away the muck left behind by the horses. Kids, laughing and dancing would kick off their shoes and run behind the cart with the water spraying out over their legs and feet.

As the war dragged on, it was not long before men started to return home, armless, legless, and limping along on canes and crutches. It was about this time mother received a telegram from Switzerland, informing her that father was in hospital. He had been on a mission behind enemy lines with a buddy tossing grenades into German foxholes. Pinned down by enemy gunfire, his mate died in the ensuing gunfight. Father lay there for two days, before he was able to find his way back to his company. Suffering from severe frostbite to both of his feet, they had to hospitalize him and amputated most of his toes.

With rumours of the war ending, people began to make plans for a grand homecoming. After all, a grateful government would abide by its promise, "A land fit for heroes to live in." However, as mother put it, when father finally limped back home in his therapeutic boots, "He was a weary, bitter, lost and disillusioned man. " and found, to his mortally wounded pride, that his King and country had no more need of him and was discharged.

The war had not improved anything for the East Enders. No signs of new housing the government had promised, unemployment was high and wages were low. When father went back to the docks, he was unable to work as well as he once could and with his malformed feet, made redundant after a few months. He did, however find a few odd jobs, helping the costermongers, sorting fruit and vegetables, with mother making pies and soup from the discarded produce. One time he had helped on a sweet stall, but that did not last long after he gave us kid's too many sweets for too little money. He did eventually find full-time work at one of the local stables.

With the addition of two more children, Timothy junior and Nora, there were now seven of us living in a two room flat at the top of the house on Marcus Street, Plaistow. Mother and father decided it was now time to move and find a larger house. Their search took them to a house in Leroy Street, with a living room and kitchen downstairs and two bedrooms upstairs, which gave everyone a little more privacy. For me, it was a dungeon of a place, running alive with all kinds of vermin. With gallons of carbolic, we gave the place a good cleaning, and two days later, mother declared it liveable. After moving in, though, it was not long before the fleas and bedbugs began to take over the place again.

On the hot summer nights, mother and father would sit outside in the street, until the early hours of the morning talking with the neighbours to escape the torture of the parasites. My brothers, sisters, and I would lie in bed and take bets on the bugs as they raced toward the ceiling. Those that lagged behind would be stuck to the wall with a pin, which was another way of getting rid of them.

Lying in bed some nights with the windows open, we could hear the adults outside chatting away about all the local gossip. This was how we knew about what scandals were going on in the neighbourhood: things kids are not suppose to know about, like miscarriages, breach births, and milk fever. In fact, this is how we found out that mother was pregnant again with her sixth child.

There were times too, when we would climb out of the back window and onto the lavatory roof to smoke old dog-ends that father had left lying around. One night, tipped off by a neighbour, father had hidden himself in the lavatory, scaring the living daylights out of us when he poked his head out over the eaves trough. Terrified, we all scrambled back up the drainpipe and into the bedroom. Hearing his footsteps coming up the stairs we screamed out for our mother as we tried to hold the door closed, to no avail. With one mighty shove, he kicked the door open, whipped off his belt and walloped the lot of us.

When families were hard up in those days, they could always go on Parish Relief. A program run by the local churches that was available to help the poor put food on the table and it was there just for the asking. Many times when mother did not know where the next meal was coming from; she would plead with father to go and seek the help we so desperately needed. Stubbornly he refused to go, saying, "I'd rather die than go cap in hand to that bunch of bloody hypocrites."

Neighbours, who had been down to the Parish Relief for help, would come past our house with pillowcases filled with bread, treacle, margarine and tea. Then their kids would come back out in the street a few minutes later with doorstep sized bread and treacle sandwiches. We would act all offhand, as if we didn't care, yet all the while, green-eyed with envy.

The Salvation Army was always our family's good old standby and kept us supplied with soup once or twice a week: one jug per person as long as you had a coupon from the local newspaper. That one jug was never enough for our family, so mother would send us out in search of old newspapers to get the extra coupons. Papers, left behind by passengers on the trams, were always a good source. We would jump on and off very quickly as the trams slowed down at their stops, much to the irritation of the conductor.

There were times when mother would send us down to the

slaughterhouse too. After severing the heads from the hides, the men would then slice the ears off and call the kids in rotation, filling their bags with the ears. Many times mother had thanked the Lord while she stood at the stove, stirring the ears in a glop broth of potatoes and onions. This was never a favourite meal for us. One time, my sister Nora almost choked on a piece of the stewed ear. As she sat there gasping for air, father hollered out to her, "Swallow it for Christ sake!" Mother, jumping up from the table, gave Nora a hard slap on the back, dislodging a large lump of ginger fur. It flew through the air and landed in the middle of the table. At this point, all spoons went down on the table as we grimaced at the disgusting scrap of hide lying there. Snatching up the grisly remnant, my father threw it in the fire, then cussing he thumped the table. "Eat," he hollered. With the crackle and stench of burning fur and gristle filling the room, we hesitantly picked up our spoons and made a feeble attempt to finish our dinner.

Living near the docks was a source of much crime. Gamblers were always willing to pay a kid to watch out for the police while they played *"Crown and Anchor"* in a back alley. As soon as a bobby showed up at the top of the street, I would skip into the alley. This would be the sign for them to scarper. With not a lot of pocket money in those days, I found it hard to explain sometimes where my extra money came from. Mother always accepted it gracefully when I told her I got it running errands; my father was always suspicious of the amount, but knew if he played his cards right with mother, there would be a beer or two at the end of the week.

Every Christmas, the local church, along with the Member of Parliament, sponsored a party for children in the neighbourhood. Standing at the entrance of the hall, we gazed in wide-eyed amazement at the abundance of cakes, biscuits and buns that awaited our ravenous little tummies. Once seated, there was much fanfare as the stage curtains opened dramatically revealing a spectacular Christmas tree. Following grace, hands shot out grabbing all that was within reach until we could eat no more. After the mandatory singing of a few Christmas carols and a "Punch and Judy Show," it was time for Santa to hand out presents. Hanging on the tree was a doll with a china face and long blonde hair that I had coveted all evening. Sitting there on Santa's knee, he gave me a little box with a broach in it fashioned in the shape of a shamrock leaf. In disbelief I looked at it, then gazing back up at the tree to the object of my affection, I gave a heartfelt plea to Santa for the doll. He then, bending over whispered in my ear what I thought might be words of comfort, "You take what you bloody well got." At home, I discreetly gave the broach to my mother. Delighted with it, she pinned it onto her blouse and touching it lovingly with her hand, smiled down at me. "It's lovely, Tilly." It was at that moment I realized that nobody had ever given mother a Christmas present. With all the struggles she had gone through to put food on the table and clothes on our back, all the washing and scrubbing she had done to keep the bugs at bay, no one had stop to think or say, "Thanks, Mum."

Christmas was not always a happy time of the year for us. It was a mystery to us why the toys we had so earnestly asked Santa for, never showed up in our stockings. One Christmas, my brother John, with his nose pressed up against the shop window had gazed longingly at a windjammer with its big white sails. He had sailed it on the pond in the park many times in his mind to the envy of all the other kids. He fretted for weeks leading up to Christmas that Santa might not get his letter, and the boat would go to some other little boy. On Christmas morning, we woke early to find rag dolls sticking out of our stockings with painted faces, not the flaxen haired porcelain dolls we had asked Santa to bring us. Digging down the stocking we would find an orange, some tired looking liquorice and then to our delight, a bright new shiny penny.

My brother John had not been so easily pleased, as he sat in utter misery, staring at a box of tin soldiers that had replaced the boat. With a few comforting words, Addy tried to sooth his disappointment, but his pent up emotion gave way to rage as he seized the box and with all his might threw it through the bedroom window. Then flinging his head into his pillow he began to sob bitterly, the tears drowning all hopes of his ever having what he had so passionately desired. He never forgot it. With the cold foggy wind gusting through the broken window, we wrapped our blankets around ourselves and ran downstairs to the warmth of the kitchen. Sitting in front of the fire with our feet propped up on the fender, father inquired as to why John looked so miserable. "He never got the boat he asked Santa for," said Addy. Father in his off the cuff manner replied, "Well maybe he couldn't read ya bloody writing."

With Christmas over with, life got back to the same old day-to-day drudgery, until one morning our parents received a letter. It had come from the court urging them to drop by at a suitable time. Puzzled by the letter, they quickly dressed, got us off to school and then made their way up to the courthouse. When we came home from school, mother ushered us all into the kitchen, sat us down at the table and brought out the letter. Reading aloud, it said that a benevolent society had awarded the family the handsome sum of ten shillings a month.

Discussing what to do with the money, mother wanted to take it and go into some type of business. When one of us suggested we go back into the produce business again, mother gave a resounding. "No thank you very much!" She had tried it once before, but now with young ones to take care of it would not be easy. As well as the round trips to the wholesaler's and back in the morning, pushing a heavy barrow over cobblestones was too strenuous. The novelty had soon worn off with us older kids too. We fought like cat and dog over whose turn it was to work on the weekends. The final straw came one Saturday, when Addy, for some unknown reason fainted, fell onto the barrow, upsetting the whole thing. Cabbage, potatoes, lettuce, tomatoes and cucumbers all spilled out into the street, just as a team of large carthorses passed by, kicking and stomping the produce into a giant pseudo looking salad. As mother stood there wringing her hands, flabbergasted at the horrific sight, she finally threw her arms in the air, turned to us and said, with a smile on her face. "I think I've had enough of this bloody business."

In retrospect, whenever she told that story we always had a good laugh over it. Father was of the same mind as mother. "No more produce barrow, time for bed, we can think on it more tomorrow," he said. That night in bed, we kids all had our own ideas on what to do with ten bob a month, and none of it involved going into business.

Returning home from school one day we found an aunt, four cousins, and a granddad we had never met before. The aunt had been living in Canada and due to matrimonial problems had decided to return to England. The aunt could not take care of granddad full time anymore and was trying to come up with an arrangement where our mother could help share the burden. Mother finally agreed that we would have him for the first four months and the aunt would take him for the next four months on a rotation bases. Gathering her brood together, she said her goodbyes and left. We never saw her again.

With an extra mouth to feed it put a sudden end to where the money would go and our hopes and plans for a brighter future. Mother had to go buy another cot and bedding for granddad and the only place to set it up was in the living room. Granddad was never happy with this arrangement. He always complained that the kids made too much noise in the morning while they were getting ready for school. He forever complained about his bed, said it was infested with fleas and he could never get any sleep at night, despite the fact mother deloused his bed every day with Keats powder before he went to bed. Kids being kids, to get back at him we would often argue in front of him, as to who would get his cot, when and if he went to the workhouse. Other times we would line up four or five mousetraps under his cot at night, before we went to bed. This would be sure to wake him sometime during the night as they snapped shut with the mice.

In order to keep granddad busy during the day and help him pay for his keep, father took some of the ten shillings from the benevolent society and bought scrap lumber. At home, mother and granddad would chop and bundle it for kindling during the day. When we came home from school, it was our job to go around the neighbourhood and sell it. With the extra money from the wood sale, and father working full time at one of the stables, the family's future looked a little brighter. With only a couple of weeks left as their part of the deal to take care of granddad, mother began to look forward to the break and a little more time for herself, that, however was not to be. While lying in bed one night, we overheard mother telling a neighbour that the aunt, who had left granddad with us, had been taken into hospital. In the course of the conversation, she mentioned that she had tried to terminate a pregnancy and died because of it.

Brothers John and Jim were both born in Leroy Street, Jim's birth had been a difficult one and it was touch and go at one point if mother was going to live. Born with a syndrome known as St.Vitas Dance, Jim had a mannerism of uncontrolled leg kicks and high-pitched crowing noises, which earned him the nicknamed of "Rooster" out on the street. This brought the total number of kids to seven, all sleeping in one room upstairs, with mother and father in the other and granddad in the living room downstairs.

Unable to care for granddad any longer, the workhouse was the only option left. As mother helped him dress that morning, I watched her as she bent down to tie his shoes, aware of mother's tears; granddad patted her on the head. "Hush Paddy, Hush now," he said. Glancing up at his face, I saw tears running down his wrinkled cheeks too. Behind him, Nora, Jim and John were rudely arguing as to who should get his bed. Father, picking up his case, began to shuffle him down the hallway. At the doorway granddad hesitated. "Was there anything else, granddad?" my father asked. Patting his pocket wherein lay his pipe and tobacco he said "Nothing else."

Addy came home from school one day and announced to mother that she was going to be a missionary. She planned to attend church regularly, study the Bible and then go to China. Mother gave her a gentle smile of indulgence and father a disgusted frown. We were gob-smacked. She had been our fearless leader, always the first to run through the fish market shooting out her hand, showing us how to stealthily snatch a fish, or run past a barrow and grab a hand full of grapes. Addy would be the first one to come to our aid if ever we were caught. Bare-facing it out with the shopkeeper, she would let them know in no uncertain terms that they had a bloody nerve accusing one of them of shoplifting.

True to her word though, Addy began attending church regularly and would sit for hours in the upstairs bedroom reading her Bible. One day she came home and told mother that when she was eighteen she would be going to Bible College to train for her missionary work in China. This was when father lost it. He grabbed a poker from the fireside and waving it in Addy's face; he threatened to swipe the head off her shoulders if he heard any more talk of China. It was not the thought of Addy going to China that had so riled father, but the fact that she would soon turn fourteen and would be eligible to work and bring home some much-needed money.

To father's aggravation, Addy continued to attend her church, in spite of our own efforts to try to get her to quit. One day we had raked all the rotten fruit out from under the barrows at the market and gone down to the church and hung around patiently while they set up for their weekly open air service. Waiting for just the right moment when the organist struck his first chord, we showered them with all of the rotten fruit. Delighted with the bedlam we had caused, we ran laughing and screaming as the pastor, hindered with a clubfoot, had run across the street trying to catch one of us.

Addy came home that night in tears as she told mother how humiliated she had been and how the man had gone on playing even when the rotten tomatoes had splashed all over his keyboard. Father, gazing into the fire and giving it a poke had no comment. Mother, who had been getting madder by the minute, gave us all a good licking and sent us to bed.

The final break from the church came a few weeks later after a picnic trip to Epping Forest. Father had given Addy strict instructions to be home by ten and mother had warned her not to upset her father. However, when ten thirty had come and she was not home, father was ready to hit the ceiling. Cussing and blinding, he marched up and down the passage, spewing out his verbal diatribe as he waited. It was just after eleven when she walked through the door, and all father's built-up emotions let go. Sitting out on the landing, we watched as he pulled off his belt and began thrashing her repeatedly as she tried to push by him to get upstairs. Mother, coming to her aid, got a backhander for her trouble that sent her sprawling into the street. With one blood-curdling scream, Addy pushed by him and ran up the stairs into the bedroom and we all flew in behind her.

Seeing my sister lying there shivering and muttering, I felt miserable about the times we had taunted her as she knelt by her bed to pray, how she had tried to bring some measure of decency into her life. Even her hopes of becoming a missionary had been ruined by the misgivings of our parents.

Creeping down the stairs at her tearful request for a drink of water, I was filled with overwhelming pity for her, when I saw the flowers she had so lovingly picked for mother laying broken and strewn along the passage. Coming back upstairs, in my heart I screamed at my father. "I hate you! I wish you were dead!" Lying there in the stillness of the night, listening to the sobs of our sister, we could hear father berating our mother for coming to Addy's defence. Then my stomach almost churned out of control when from out of the darkness of the room, Tim yelled out, "I'm gonna kill you one day, you old bastard!" He never did, but Tim did break father's jaw one time when he came to the defence of our mother.

Returning home from school one day, we found the house in darkness and the fire was out. Tim went to the cupboard for some coal to start a fire, but found none. I fumbled for a match to light the gas, but the meter had run out. With no gas or coal, we all sat there in the cold and dark. With the wind whistling down the chimney and the sound of mice scurrying across the floor we sank further under our blankets in an effort to keep warm. We were on the verge of somnolence, when there was a fumbling at the front door, and then the sound of our mother's voice came from the passage, "Where are you all?" Scampering out from under the blankets, we ran to greet her. Father came in behind her and threw a small bag of coal down by the fire. After replenishing the gas meter with a penny, mother knelt down at the hearth and began to set a fire. There was an atmosphere of foreboding in the air as father asked if there was anything to eat. "There's nothing", mother said quietly through tight lips. "I've enough for fish and chips," said father. "I'm not hungry," she replied. "You haven't eaten all day", he said. "And I ain't likely to eat all day tomorrow either!" she fired back. "Well for Christ sake!" he exploded and slammed his fist on the table. Snatching his hat from off a nail on the back of the door, he rushed out of the house.

It was not until our sister Addy returned home from the pictures, that we found out the reason for mother's displeasure. Noticing the empty barrow sitting outside, on her way in, Addy had asked where the wood was. "There be no more wood, and what's more there be no more money." The finality of my mother's words filled us all with dismay as she spoke. "They said someone in high authority thought that we were wasting the money buying wood." "But didn't you tell them what we were doing with it?" asked Addy. "They told us they would take another look at it in six months," said mother. "Good God, what are we suppose to do until then?" asked Addy. "I just don't know," said mother, "But I doubt we'll ever get the money back again," she said sadly. "Why ever not mother?" asked Addy. "Why not, I'll tell you why not, because your father told them just where they could shove their bloody money." "For love of heaven," said Addy. "Trust him to go put his foot in it."

Mother had always accepted poverty with a fierce stoicism, and knowing that things could not get much worse, had always buoyed her hopes of a brighter tomorrow.

Chapter 2

Tumbridge Wells

...if you go a hopping, hopping down in Kent
you'll see old mother Riley putting up a tent...

A letter in the post this morning from the Town Hall concerning re-housing had set mother and father off in a tizzy. They quickly dressed and hurried out of the house and down to the office in anticipation of moving to a new house. Returning later that day, they were filled with excitement. The council were going to build a new housing estate at Downham, in Kent. Their name was near the top the list for a move. "We're going to live in a new house in the country," said mum catching her breath, "Enough room for a bit of a garden, where I can grow a few vegetables and flowers." "Maybe get another produce wagon," father jested. "They got electric lights in every room," said mum joyfully. "What's electric light?" asked Nora. Mum looking puzzled, "I'm not sure, but the man said all you have to do is just flick a switch on the wall and the lights come on." With no idea of how electricity worked, our parents were unable to explain the concept to us. All mother knew is that there would be no more gaslights to play with. "Sounds like a magic house," said Tim. "Indoor lavatory too, and a bathtub with hot and cold running water!" exclaimed father. With no set timetable for the move to Downham, the excitement of that day quickly passed and life slipped back into its everyday drudgery.

It was about this same time father had a visit from his sister Alice. She had just received her letter from a hop farm in Kent, the same farm she went to each year for hop picking. They had invited her back for another season of picking. Unable to go this time, she thought that father might like to take the family in her place. "A chance for you to get out of the city, Tim," she said, "away from the smog and pollution, get some clean fresh air in your lungs." Mother, who had sat listening to the conversation, needed no persuading, but waited anxiously for father's response.

Having a letter and a free train pass from a farm inviting you back for another hop-picking season, was like having a ticket to a holiday camp for some Londoners. It was always a major topic of discussion down at the local pub this time of year as to who had received their letter. They could now be part of that conversation. Mother was overjoyed when father finally said we could go. With the prospect of earning a few extra bob, she threw her arms around father and gave him a big hug, a show of affection rarely seen between the two of them.

Mother loved to sing, and her demeanour could always be measured by how a song resonated with her. If she was annoyed or upset, she could be very quiet. If she were contemplative, she would hum. If she were happy, she could sing the whole daylong. This was the case as she began packing. She sang for two days straight, with father telling her to, "Pipe down," occasionally. While mother stuffed boxes with extra clothes, pots, pans and bedding, things we would need for a month away from home, father spent his time fixing up his cart; repairing wheels, greasing the axels and strengthening the handlebars. On Saturday morning, we were up early to help father load the cart, while mother fixed food and poured pots of hot tea into glass bottles for our journey. The young ones, eager to get going, ran up and down the street with much excitement in anticipation of their first train ride. Father, finishing his smoke, flicked the butt into the gutter and checked the straps on the cart one more time. Giving them a final tug, he hollered, "Let's get!" and we were on our way.

There was much good-natured banter with the neighbours as we made our way up the cobblestone street. At the top of the road, we joined a convoy of other pickers making their way to the station. Barrow boys along the way shouted out their warnings to the young girls, cautioning them about farm boys. "Watch out for those yobo's down in Kent," said one. "Keep ya hand on ya ha'penny," said another. They in return, with indifference, threw them sardonic kisses.

At the station, the women stood round discussing the latest gossip, while grandparents scolded children as they ran around, jumping over suitcases and climbing on the benches. The men gathered at the far end of the platform for a smoke, ready to load the carts onto the baggage car.

When the train finally arrived, I was shocked at what I saw. This was not one of the elegant looking express trains we had seen making its way over to the continent; no elaborate coaches, fancy headrests and napkins holders, it was the most awful train I had ever seen. There were vulgar words scrawled in the dirt on the windows and large rust patches with the paint flaking off. Inside the coaches were small wooden benches to sit on. Cigarette butts, and newspapers littered the floor, and the pungent odour of urine permeated the carriage.

Mother quickly found a place to sit, and put the baby on her knee, while father hastily placed our bags in the overhead rack and found a seat. With a wave of the porter's flag and a blast of the whistle, doors slammed shut. A rowdy cheer sounded down the length the train as it rattled out of the station. Soon the beer began to flow and a rousing chorus of; *"Old Mother Riley"* rang out. Standing glued to the windows, kids watched as the industrial backyards of London gave way to blocks of slum flats and then a leisurely transition out of the city and into the countryside of Kent. Fields of golden wheat waved in the breeze, men bringing in the harvest and orchards with trees loaded down with apples. Cows and sheep grazing in green pastures, country cottages dotting the landscape, and an unfettered view of the sky, blue as I had ever seen, stretching as far as I could see.

At noon, mother cut up a loaf of bread, and placed a large chunk of cheese on top to fill our bellies and for a treat, arrowroot biscuits, all washed down with a bottle of lukewarm sugary tea. After lunch, the men now fortified with beer, laughingly held up sheets for the women, as without shame they took a pee in a pot. Having done their good deed, the men then directed the women and children to look in the opposite direction, while they relieved themselves out the window. With young Jim feeling the urge to relieve himself, father took the pot back down from the luggage rack and directed him to pee into it. When he had finished, father went to throw it out the window but the wind caught it, blowing it back in his face. "Foocking hell!" father yelled "Look at me now; I'm all covered in piss . . . for Christ Sake. Nobody better go again till we get off this train, yer hear."

Pulling into the station at Tumbridge Wells, we joined the mass exodus of pickers leaving the train, each family checking in with their various farms. We quickly found our group and checked in with the tallyman and then we were off down the road to our farm with about ten other families.

With the tall grass and bracken growing along the roadside, we could not help running through it, laughing and giggling as it tickled our arms and legs. Then falling headfirst into the hedge-grove-jungle, we would disappear out of sight. Local yokels sat on farm gates, teasing the young girls as we walked by, and they in return patted their backsides in mockery, sending the young men off in howls of laughter.

About a mile down the road, we cut across a field toward a group of small, whitewashed huts. Here the bailiff was waiting to welcome us. Allotting the hut numbers, he told parents to keep their kids out of the orchards, and the men told there was to be no poaching. After a brief run down on what time the farm whistle would blow and where we were to meet on Monday, he mounted his horse and rode off.

Before moving into our hut mother gave the place a good sweep, I ran to fetch a bucket of water, ready for her to wash the floor. Father sent the other kids in search of firewood for the stove, while he made up the straw mattresses. After giving the place a good clean, mother hauled the cart over to our hut and began to unpack. In preparation for dinner, I grabbed another pot of water and began to peel the potatoes.

After dinner, our folks joined some of the neighbours and we took a walk down to the local pub. Here, publicans greeted returning hop-pickers like family. While our parents enjoyed a night out at the pub, we ran barefooted and wild over the village green, throwing ourselves down in the grass and smelling the sweet clover. The local kids looked on perplexed. They must have thought we were all a little demented.

Stepping out of the pub at closing time and into the darkness of the night, mothers called out in earnest for their children. Then, when all were gathered and accounted for, we headed back to the huts. A harvest moon rode high in a partially clouded sky, alternately lighting a ghostly landscape and then plunging it into darkness. Older kids taunted the younger ones with eerie ghost stories, reaching out and touching them with wraithlike fingers, setting them off in shrieks of fright. The only other sounds that night were of several stragglers as they gave a few rousing courses of, *"Maybe it's because I'm a Londoner..."*

Back at the hut, mother lit the oil lamp and we undressed in its warm pale glow and climbed into our straw beds. Up since six o'clock that morning, it had been a long active day, and with the sweet smell of sackcloth and the rustle of our straw mattresses, we drifted off to sleep.

I woke early Sunday morning to the sounds of the men outside the huts as they went through their morning ritual. Sloshing the water down the drain and putting their buckets down noisily. Lying there in the cool of the morning, I decided I would surprise everyone by getting up early and making breakfast. Dressing silently, I tiptoed to the cupboard, took out some kippers, a loaf of bread and some margarine. Outside, I put a pot on the open fire to make the tea and laid the knives and forks out on the cart that doubled as our table. While the kippers sizzled in the fry pan, I sliced and toasted the bread. When all was ready, I crept back into the hut and stood in the centre of the room. Then with my best rendition of Billy Cotton, from *"The Billy Cotton Band Show,"* I banged on a pot and bellowed, "Wakey wakey! Come and get it!" Well I got it all right. My father leapt out of bed and with one swift back hander, knocks me sideways toward the door. "Ya daff cow!" he yelled. "Now look what ya gone and done. Ya woke the baby." Yelling back at him as I flew out the door, "The baby was already awake!"

Running to the far side of the meadow, I was angry, upset and full of self-pity; I told myself it wasn't fair, after all the trouble I had gone through to get breakfast for them all too. Here I was, walking around in the dew-covered grass, wet, cold and hungry. The only consolation I had was that my father would be going back to London this afternoon for the week. With that in mind, I wandered the lanes around the farm until I knew for sure he would be gone. I then made my way back to the compound. Arriving at the hut, I found it locked and the place deserted. Everyone had gone to town to see their kinfolks off on the train back to London. Weary, tired and with aching feet, I sat on a gate, my eyes fixated down the road looking for any sign of my mother returning. With the sound of a train whistle in the distance, I knew she would soon be on her way home. Jumping off the gate, I ran down the lane towards town to meet her. On the way back home mother questioned me about my day. She was quiet and withdrawn, almost aloof as she listened to my answers. I do not think she was angry with me. It was father and his unwarranted temper that had cast such a dismal gloom over Sunday.

Back at the hut, she gave me a plate of cold meat and potatoes. After she tucked us all up in bed, I watched as she silently packed the bags that we would need for the hop fields in the morning. Then wearily, she climbed into the bed beside me and before laying her head down on the pillow, she reached out and ruffled my hair. "That was a lovely breakfast ya made this morning Tilly," she said, bringing a tear of relief to my eye as she spoke.

At six o'clock, the farm whistle blew and mother jumped out of the bed, lit the fire, got tea on the go and then made a large pot of porridge. Keen to get started, we were up and out of bed, dressed, and had our breakfast. After porridge, toast and tea we were ready for our first day in the field. We had never picked hops before and had no idea what to expect. Mother, however, had set a quota for us to fill before we could go play. The first day, in our enthusiasm, we picked hard and fast and duly impressed her, by filling our quota by noon. Setting a level, we would have to live up to the rest of the season. As the days went by and our eagerness dwindled, we found it hard to get up in the morning, especially on rainy days when the hops would be wet, slippery and hard to pick. Filling our quota for the day became a real chore. There were days too when it was hard to stay focused on picking hops, especially when we watched the other kids running around and playing, or enjoying a ride on the wagon as it went back and forth to the Oast Houses. However, a good clip along side the ear from mother, would quickly bring us back to the task. Working away during the day, mother would pass the time by singing along with her fellow pickers, or reflecting on the things she would need to buy with the extra money; new boots and coats for the kids, extra coal for the winter, a tin bathtub or maybe a new mattress. To keep our spirits up, she would promise us rabbit stew for dinner on Sundays.

With the faint hint of fall in the air, hopping season began to wind down and all that remained in the fields was the skeletal remains of the poles and wire. Working the final section of the field, a loud cheer went up from all the pickers as they pulled the last of the bines. Then, in the age-old ritual, there were the screams of protest from the women, as the men chased them around the field and threw them into the hop bins. Even the tallymen were unable to avoid a dunk in the bin and took it all in good fun. There would be one more good night out at the pub, and then back to the hut to start packing for our journey home.

In the morning, we were up early to load the cart for mother. Father had not shown up as he had promised, to help mother with the journey back home. Closing the hut door, mother scanned the fields one last time in hopes she might see father coming across the pasture. With no sign of him, she grabbed the handles of the cart and we helped her wheel it across the field. At the farm, the bailiff gave mother a final pay package and thanked her for a good job. Taking the cash, she carefully recounted it, then securing it in a handkerchief, slid it down the front of her blouse. On the way into Tumbridge, a flock of sheep passing along the lane had slowed our progress. Lost in thought while watching the dog and shepherd work their magic, mother almost jumped out of her skin when father came up behind her and grabbed her by the arm. "Where ya bin?" he grumped. "I've been looking all over for ya." "Here just a minute!" she said irritably, "Don't forget I had all the packing to do."

In town, we stopped by the pub for lunch before catching the train home to London. "Well how did you make out then?" Father asked. Mother, now warming up to him, "Well, I've made enough for coats and boots for the kids and if there's some leftover, a little extra coal for the winter." She had done better than she let on, wanting to keep a little in reserve. Sitting there, enjoying the fruits of her labour, her world fell apart as father spoke again. "I'm not working," he said. Unable to believe what she had heard, "What do ya mean not working? What the hell happened then? Did you get laid-off at the stables?" "No, I quit. I'm going back to the docks," he said. With the sudden realization that all her hard work was for naught, tears filled her eyes. "That means there won't be any new coats or boots for the kids, you selfish bastard!" she sobbed. With that, father finished his beer, banged the glass down on the table, "Let's get," he scoffed and headed out the door for the station.

It was a depressing journey back home. Mother sat in the corner of the coach with her eyes closed, not saying a word. It was in stark contrast to a month ago when we had set out on the train in light-hearted camaraderie with our fellow pickers and with high expectations. Gazing out the window now at this peaceful countryside, I began to compare the carefree days of the past month, with the miserable slum streets of London. Instead of being plagued by fleas, mother had laughed along with us at the tickling of the straw as it poked through the mattress. In the evening, soft breezes drifted across the meadow, with the tangy scent of hops drying in the kilns, a stark contrast to the stench of urine and dung that fouled our hopscotch and permeated our home in Leroy Street. Yet we had skipped with wild abandon over the cow paddies that littered the fields on our way to pick hops; laughing at the misfortunes of one poor kid who, one day, slipped and sat down in a fresh one. A scolding by the farmer for scrumping a few apples was far sweeter to our ears than the sounds of our bullying father.

Back in London, life went on pretty much as it had done in the past. Coats and boots from the Sally Ann, cow ears from the slaughterhouse and a bit of coal pinched from here and there. Father's job at the docks fell through, with the younger men chosen over him for what little work there was. This left him doing odd jobs and mother scratching away to make a few extra pennies with her sewing. We did go back hop picking for a few more seasons, until some of us began to leave school and find our own way. Eventually we did move to Downham where Nelly was born, she was the eighth and the last of the Regan clan. Mother brought Granddad home from the workhouse and he lived out the rest of his days in relative peace and quiet in the country. Addy was the first to marry, then Rose. Jim and John ran away to sea as soon as they were able and ended up serving in the American Merchant Navy. After the Second World War, Jim settled down in Australia and John made his way to Canada. Tim, Nora, Nell, and I stayed close to home, and looked after our mother, who was in poor health. She passed away suddenly in 1938, of a heart attack, at the age of fifty-two. A beloved mother who had stood tall in the face of many adversities, and instilled in us the will to work, as if she had foreseen the turbulent times that would lay ahead for one of her brood. I worked as a waitress and eventually took an apprenticeship to become a cook. Tim went into plumbing and became a master pipe fitter. Nora tried a few things, but never stuck with much in the way of a career, she soon married her long time boy friend, Reg, a nary-do-well gypper. Nelly eventually moved in with Reg and Nora who had rented a small acreage at Rainham and were planning to go into market gardening.

Chapter 3

Holland

*When the need is the highest,
salvation is the nearest.*

Old Dutch Proverb

In 1939, at the age of thirty, Tilly was two years into her cook's apprenticeship at a London restaurant. At the time, the dark clouds of war were starting to gather over Europe. In September of that year, the Nazi German invasion of Poland was the catalyst that touched off the Second World War. With the outbreak of war, women were called on to fill the void left by the men as they went off to fight. Following her mother's example, Tilly put her cook training on hold and went to work in a munitions factory in London. Like many other women, she felt the strength of pride and duty to do her part for the war effort.

While working in London, Tilly met and fell in love with a young soldier. They made plans to marry as soon as all the madness was over. One day, while looking for a wedding dress, she noticed a *"For sale"* sign in a shop window advertising a wedding dress. After making enquiries, the young girl told Tilly that she bought the dress from a friend whose fiancée was missing in action. She had planned to marry in a few months herself, but her future husband had died in a bomb attack on London. She now, no longer needed or wanted the dress. Tilly purchased it with the hope that sometime soon she would be the one to be married in it. Not long after the purchase though, her hopes and dreams came to a sudden end. On a weekly visit, her future mother-in-law informed Tilly that her son Peter had been killed in a bomb attack on London. With a similar heartbreak story, Tilly now posted the same ad for the dress that she had read just a few months before.

Living in a small rooming house in London, Tilly was left alone to grieve the loss of Peter. When she returned to her job at the munitions factory, life went back to its daily grind for her. Until one day, after Tilly had left work for the day, the afternoon shift at the munitions factory took a direct hit from German bombs, killing many of her fellow workers. With the loss of her mother, her fiancée and now her co-workers, Tilly was at her wits end with the stress and torment of war, felt she needed a break from all the bombing and killing in London.

Giving up her job in munitions, she moved out to Pitsea to stay with her sister Rose for a time. While there, she went to work at Shell Haven cleaning out oil storage tanks. To access the inside of these tanks, workers would need to climb through a small manhole at the bottom. Once inside, workers would slip and slide around on the scum as they cleaned the sludge from the bottom of the reservoirs. Because of the fumes, workers were only allowed inside for a short periods. With the Shell petroleum refinery close by, it was a particularly dangerous job, as the refinery was a major target during the battle of Britain. With the sound of an air raid siren, there would be a mad dash as workers scrambled to get out through the manhole and into an air raid shelter.

On weekends, the Barge and Tavern in Pitsea were popular pubs for service men, and women to have a good time and forget about the trials and troubles of the war. In the Barge one evening, while out with some friends, Tilly first met Simon, a Dutch Merchant Navy seaman working on supply convoys going between Halifax and London. Taken by Simon's natural good looks and charm, they were both infatuated with each other. They met a few more times over the course of the war whenever Simon was on leave in England. It was on one of these occasions that Simon proposed to Tilly, just before he shipped out on one of his convoys. Although Simon was five years younger than Tilly, she had made up her mind to marry him. While she did not accept the proposal at that time, she told him she would think about it and let him know her answer when and if he returned.

The Allied Merchant Fleets were keeping the British population supplied with food and fuel in those threatening days, with the Dutch and Norwegian ships taking the biggest losses. After a three-month absence, and with that statistic in mind, Tilly thought that Simon might have met the same fate as Peter. On the other hand, was he just simply having second thoughts about marriage? When he finally did make an appearance, much to Tilly's relief, she accepted his proposal of marriage.

On August 25th 1944, Matilda Maud Regan married Simon Roders in a garden ceremony at her sister Rose's home in Timber Log Lane, Pitsea. After a short honeymoon, Simon returned to his ship and spent the rest of the war in Egypt and North Africa.

Back at sea, Simon received word that the winter of 1944-45 had been one of the coldest winters of the war in Holland. With the freezing temperatures and the lack of food and fuel due to the German occupation, many civilians were dying from the cold and starvation. With the shortage of food, many of the soup kitchens in the towns and villages were forced to close, the young and the elderly suffering the most. Estimates ranged in the tens of thousands of citizens dying of malnutrition during the five-year long occupation. By the end of the war, most of the Jewish population had been shipped out of Holland to Nazi concentration camps in Germany; once there they were systematically exterminated in the gas ovens.

In the meantime, Eisenhower had brokered a food bombardment program with the Germans. This allowed the allies to drop food parcels to the starving population of

Holland. Dubbed "Operation Manna" the sight and sound of American and British bombers from England flying low over the towns and cities of Holland, was music to the Dutch people's ears. They watched in wonder as the precious food supplies began dropping by parachute. Still concerned for his aging parents though, Simon began to make plans to get in touch with them on his next trip back to England.

An Old Dutch proverb, *"When the need is the highest the salvation is nearest."* was about to come true for the people of Holland. On May 7, 1945, with the food armistice in full operation, the German army surrendered Holland. The Nazi brute having lost its stranglehold on Holland, would soon loose its grip of oppression on the rest of world. With much jubilation, the Dutch rejoiced along with their Canadian, American and British liberators, pouring into the streets hugging and kissing each other and waving flags. With the liberation of Holland and reports that the Port of Rotterdam had been reopened, allowing food shipments to enter, eased Simon's mind somewhat. However, he still had concerns for his mother and fathers well being.

With the war now ending, Simon was set to do his last tour of duty. Arriving back in England on a short leave, Tilly greeted him with the news that she was pregnant and the baby was due sometime in June. Simon had mixed feelings about fatherhood. He had spent most of his working life in the army and then the navy. Returning soon to civilian life in his war-torn homeland, he was anxious about the prospects for work. Tilly, puzzled by Simon's indifference toward parenthood; was also a little surprised by the fact he intended to move back to Holland. She had never really considered the reality of leaving England to live in Holland. After a couple of days of intense discussion and planning between the two of them, Simon decided he would stay in England until the baby was born.

On June the 26th 1945 at Writtle Park Hospital Essex, Karen Adela was born. Back at sea, it would be two months after Karen's birth that Simon would see her for the first time. Upon seeing his daughter though, his attitude toward parenting changed and Simon doted on his little girl.

Tilly's youngest sister Nell was now living up in Rainham with her sister Nora, who had recently married her long-time boyfriend, Reg. During a visit one day, Nora showed Tilly and Simon a new enterprise Reg and she were working on. It was a small market garden to grow tomatoes. In postwar England, there were a few prospects opening up for this type of enterprise, and Reg wanted to get in on the ground floor. Being a bit of a wheeler-dealer, he had borrowed money from here and there to get the business up and running. In the Barge one night, over a couple of beers, Reg offered Simon a job if he were interested. It would be a low wage to start with, so Reg could put money back into the farm and grow the business. If at some time Simon were interested, he could invest and become a partner. After talking it over with Tilly, who thought it might be a good opportunity, Simon went ahead and started working for Reg. Tilly thought that Simon's partnership in a potentially successful business would help persuade him to stay in England.

For a while Nora, Reg and Simon worked well together until things got busy enough to start hiring workers. Reg, having a persuasive nature, took on the sales and marketing end of things and looked after the books. Simon took care of the construction, maintenance and delivery of greenhouse produce to market. Nora was in charge of planting, harvesting and later, staffing for the greenhouses. In his sales capacity,

Reg began to spend a lot more time looking for new markets, making business contacts and talking with wholesalers. With the rapid growth in the business, they started to break into the London market. With an increase in trade, they decided to grow a few more varieties; lettuce, peppers and cucumbers, all helped add to sales. With the growth, there came an increase in revenue. Reg now convinced Simon that this would be an opportune time for him to invest in the business. With prospects looking good, Simon went ahead and took part of his navy pension to invest in the business.

With the growth however, came the complexities involved in market gardening: tomato blight, fungus on the peppers and increases in the cost and labour. Reg in his capacity as the bookkeeper began to miss bill payments and paydays. Pickers with the increased workload, and longer hours became discontent with the missed wages and started to refuse the work. Delivery drivers too, declined to pick up produce due to lack of payment. Simon now spent most of his time planting, harvesting, taking produce to market, that he found little time for maintenance. With the increased workload, he started having differences with Nora on the day-to-day running of the farm. Reg convinced Simon that it was all just growing pains, and persuaded him to hang in; markets were opening up in London, and things would work out.

With Nora now refusing to work because of the conflict and nonexistent staff, Simon found himself working more and more by himself. With problems continuing to mount at the farm, Simon was more convinced that a move back to Holland would be in his best interest. He would talk to Reg and get him to buy back his share of the farm.

It was on one such day, while at work, Simon was preparing

to take a shipment of produce to the train for delivery to London, that the bailiff came by and served him with a lien on the farm. Nothing was to leave the property. For Simon, this was the last straw, and he made his way over to Reg's house. Knocking on the door, he found only Nell at home. She informed him that Reg and Nora were up in London for the day.

Reg, on the sly had made plans for Nora, Nell and himself to immigrate to Canada. A good deal of his time spent in London had been for organizing passports, filling out forms and doing immigration interviews at Canada House. All the profits from the farm had gone into Reg's pocket for their voyage to the "land of opportunity." By the time Simon had tracked Reg down, he had done a quick "bunk" out of the country on the fast track to Canada. No doubt sipping a cold one in the ship's lounge and counting his cash.

With the failure of the farm, bill collectors on his case and the loss of part of his pension, Simon became extremely downcast. Bitter about being left holding the bag and trying to explain the situation to clients and creditors, he began to blame Tilly for talking him into going into business with Reg. It was at this time she started to see a side of Simon she did not care for. He became increasingly more abusive, both verbally and physically.

Before long, unemployed and stressed out over the failed business, Simon made plans to return to Holland. After a particularly bad fight, he packed his bags, and left. With his mind now set on living back in Holland, nothing was going to sway him from his plan. Two weeks later, Tilly received a letter from him, with money inside for tickets. On the back of the envelope, he had scrawled the address of where he was staying. Having lived in England all her life, Tilly was not overjoyed with the prospect of moving to a foreign country, although, after five long years of war and the fiasco with Reg and Nora over the farm, Holland, she hoped, would offer her some normality in life.

Jim and John, her two brothers were now settled abroad. Tim the younger brother was still single and working on his apprenticeship as a pipe fitter. Addy was married and living up in Dagenham with her husband, Jack and their two girls, Joan and Pat. Rose had married Barry Lacey. They had a baby girl, Helen, and were now expecting a second child. Rose also had granddad Regan living with them. Things had gone well for everyone and they had all come out of the war relatively unscathed except for the loss of their mother.

It was now Tilly's turn, time for her to make a life for herself, Simon and Karen. After packing suitcases, she made her way over to Rose's to say good-bye. She then left England with a heavy heart and an uneasiness of what might lay ahead for her in Holland.

Arriving at The Hague, Tilly and Karen took a bus to Rotterdam. Here she found a bombed out shell of a city. Its citizens, physical exhausted from five long years of occupation. Cities and towns with their quaint seventeenth century architecture and newer buildings were now bombed out ruins, pulled apart by the people looking for fuel as they tried to keep warm. The children and the elderly, with their rickety bodies, showed the signs of a starvation diet. Fertile farmland reclaimed from the sea after centuries of struggle, now flooded by the Germans as they blew up the dykes that had held back the sea. The picturesque landscapes with its many canals, windmills and tulip fields, were now back under water. Greenhouses, some with their tops barely visible above the waterline twinkle in the sunlight, a sign that seemed to suggest that not all was lost. Holland was such a quiet, peace-loving country, with honest hard working people, what had they done to deserve such a fate?

At the Rotterdam bus station, Tilly took a taxi to the address Simon had scribbled on the back of the envelope: 88 Blokland Straat. It was a rough row house residence showing the signs of neglect due to the five-year long occupation. Standing outside on the street, with an uneasy feeling Tilly went up the steps and knocked on the door, expecting Simon to open it. She was surprised when a rather elderly woman opened the door. "Tilly," she said, and motioned for her to come in. In her broken English, she introduced herself as Hanna and her husband as Jake. Tilly assumed that this must be her mother and father in-law and introduced herself and Karen. Putting the kettle on for tea, Hanna indicated in her broken English that Simon would be home soon.

They were an elderly couple who spoke no English. Thin and gaunt, they too showed signs of the long German occupation. Except for short little utterances between themselves, they spoke very little to each other and seemed to have very little joy in their lives. Whenever Karen cried or fussed, there was no attempt to pick her up, or comfort her.

Simon came home at six o'clock and it was obvious to Tilly he had been at the pub as he attempted to explain the living conditions to her. Unable to find permanent work or a place to live, he had moved in with his parents, a situation he assured Tilly was only temporary. He had rented a converted railcar for them to live in; however, they would not be able to move in for another month.

Meanwhile, during the day while Simon was out looking for work, there was very little communication between Tilly and her in-laws. However, with her limited ability to speak the language, Tilly did make an effort to get out and shop for food. A cheap meal for them would be *"Boerenkoolstamppot met worst,"* (Bangers and Mash) which was served two or three times a week. When Simon came home, most of the conversation would be in Dutch. There were times when discussions around the dinner table would get a little heated between Simon and his parents. Tilly, enquiring as to what all the fuss was about, was told by Simon to mind her own business. She could only assume that it had something to do with the little amount of food they had on rations and the fact there was five of them living in a one bedroom flat

The one bedroom flat gave everyone very little privacy, but enough apparently for Tilly to get pregnant again. The thought of another mouth to feed and no steady work only added to Simon's frustration. Discontent with the state of his life, he became more irritable and argumentative with his parents. He was also increasingly more violent with Tilly, both mentally and physically. Tilly had vowed many years ago that she would never put up with brutality from a man in her life, having grown up in a home with an abusive father.

After six weeks of living with the in-laws, they finally moved into the converted railcar. With no inside plumbing, Tilly was not looking forward to caring for two small children in such cramped quarters. Glad though, finally to be out of the in-laws flat and into her own place; she was ready to make the coach a home.

With the move, Tilly was about to find out just how cruel Simon could be. In the navy, Simon had been in a position of authority. Now in his own home, his navy way of doing thing began to spill over into his private life. Things he would never have taken the liberty of while at his parent's home, he did with Tilly in their home. Meals had to be on the table at a specific time and a clean shirt every day, ironed with no creases in the sleeves. When he came home, he would run his finger along the furniture, checking for dust to see if the place had been cleaned that day. If Karen started fussing while Simon was sleeping, Tilly would have to take her out of the coach so as not to wake him. Anytime something was not to his satisfaction, there would be an argument that usually ending up with a physical beating. The fact that Tilly was pregnant at the time did not seem to bother him.

Simon's sister, Joanna, who had witnessed some of these violent outbursts, tried to persuade Tilly that the reason for Simon's abusive ways, was that he did not need or want another mouth to feed. If she were to maybe, get an abortion, things might settle down somewhat between them. Tilly, not sure if there was some complicity between Simon and Joanna, found the idea unthinkable and promptly distanced herself from Joanna. Tilly had her little girl. Now she was looking forward to the possibly of having a boy and in her own mind, she had already settled on the name of John.

As the months rolled by and her pregnancy was coming to term, Tilly did her best to keep the peace. Although she new in her heart that if things did not improve she was going to leave Simon.

On the July 5 th 1946, at 88 Blokland Straat, while having tea with her in-laws and sharing a few laughs with a good friend Riet, Tilly went into labour. With no time or chance of making it to the hospital, Riet stepped in to act as midwife. It was here at her in-law's flat that Tilly got her wish, a baby boy. Simon John James was born. Hanna sent Jake to look for Simon, to let him know Tilly was at their home and that he had a son. When my father finally arrived home, he was pleased to see he had a son, and there and then decided that my name would be Simon, after him. My mother went along for the time being, knowing in her mind that the matter of my name had not been settled. She would discuss it again with Simon later.

The night before the christening at the Seaman's Church in Noordzingel, my mother brought up the question of my name once again. She did not mind Simon, but would prefer John. With a look of disregard, my father told her that it would be Simon, end of story. She could have John James as second names, but Simon was to be my name and that was final.

With my name now settled, things did take on a more domestic atmosphere. My father had been working full time for the past six months, which meant my mother would now have two young ones to keep quiet at night while he slept. She also suspected that she might be pregnant again, but was not ready to tell my father.

With a third child on the way, my mother's thoughts turned to finding a larger place to live. After the evening meal and with Simon in a reasonably good mood, she introduced the subject of finding a bigger place. My father, quite happy to be living where he was, questioned my mother as to why she was not happy in the coach. "Rents cheap, its all we can afford right now, so what's your problem? Tilly!" Before she could tell him that she thought she might be pregnant again, and that they would need a bigger place, he flew into a rage. Telling my mother if she was not happy living in Holland, she could "piss-off" back to England as quickly as she liked," and with that he landed her a backhander. For my mother that was the last straw.

The next morning as she was making plans to leave my father, a telegram arrived from her sister Rose in England informing her that Helen, Roses daughter was very sick. Rose wanted to know if it was possible for my mother to come and help her look after her young son Jim and grandpa Regan while she dealt with her daughter Helen. My mother took this as an opportunity to have a break from Simon. After she explained the situation to my father, he suggested that it might be easier for her if she took me to England with her and left Karen with him and her Oma and Opa in Holland.

Back in England, my mother made her way over to her sister Rose's place in Pitsea. There, she found that Helen had taken a turn for the worst and was in the intensive care unit at Billericay hospital. After two weeks in the hospital, she passed away. Rose and Barry, devastated by this turn of events, relied heavily on my mother to help look after their son Jim and grandpa Regan while they made funeral arrangements. Grandma Regan, who had passed away just before the war was buried at St. Michael's church in Pitsea. It was decided that Helen would be interred along side her grandma. The day before the funeral, my mother received a telegram from Simon. In it, he told my mother that he wanted a divorce and that she was not to bother coming back to Holland. She could stay in England with John and he would keep Karen with him in Holland.

That afternoon my mother showed Rose the telegram from Simon threatening to keep Karen in Holland. She told Rose that she was sure this was the end of her marriage, but if it was the last thing she did, she must return to Holland and get Karen. Rose understood the situation and with plans for the funeral complete for the following day, she thanked my mother for all she had done. The following morning we caught the first ferry back to Holland.

I can only imagine my mothers' dread at having to go back

to Holland, face my father, and come to some resolution over Karen. Knowing his violent temper, she was not sure how, or if she should tell him that she was pregnant again. Could they come to some kind of resolution on their marriage? If they could not, how would she manage to get out of the Holland with Karen? It was with all these questions running through my mothers mind that she exited the taxi, and found herself once again standing outside 88 Blokland Straat.

Hanna answered the door, and showing no emotion, enquired as to my mothers business. She explained to Hanna that she had come to see Karen, and would like to speak to Simon. She told my mother that Simon was not at home right now. There was an awkward silence between the two of them before she finally told my mother she could come in and wait. Inside the flat she found Karen, who was happy to see her mother and brother, but it was evident too, that she had bonded with her Oma and Opa.

Simon came home just after six o'clock, showing no emotion toward my mother or me, apparently. It was clear to her though; that Karen and her dad had bonded, as they were both excited to see each other. After the evening meal that night, my mother asked the in-laws if they could take Karen and me for a walk while she and Simon talked.

Sitting at the table, my mother started by telling Simon that she was sorry for the way things had turned out. She needed to come back and see if they could try to make another go of their marriage. A situation he seemed to be pondering, until my mother told him that she was pregnant again. Taken aback and a little shocked by this news, he sat for a minute contemplating what he had just heard. He then went into a jealous rage wanting to know who the god-dam father was. My mother tried to explain to him that she was pregnant before she left Holland. However, without waiting, or wanting to hear anymore, he leaned across the table to where she sat and called her a "dirty rotten whore," then giving her a backhander so hard, it knocked her off the chair and onto the floor. Staggered and bleeding from the mouth and nose, my mother pulled herself back to her feet, looking for an explanation for his actions. Again, he began his verbal assault, telling her not to come crawling back to him with some other man's kid. Then as he started to come at her again, my mother picked up a chair and waving it in his face, tried to protect herself. Grabbing the legs of the chair, my father let out with a swift kick that caught my mother in the stomach, causing her to double up in pain and fall back onto the settee. He then threw the chair in her direction and went to leave, at the door he stopped, turned around and told her she could "fuck off back to England, back to your boyfriend as quick as you like," and left the flat, slamming the door behind him. This would be the last time my mother would ever set eyes on Simon.

Emotionally spent, she was still lying on the settee in pain when the in-laws returned home sometime later with Karen and me. There was no need for them to ask what had happened. Hanna put the kettle on and made a pot of tea. Feeling a sharp stabbing pain in her back and the need to go to the toilet, my mother got up and went into the bathroom. It was there that she suffered the miscarriage of her third child.

It was a pitiful, but thankful end to their marriage. My father never returned to the flat that night while my mother was there. The next day, exhausted after a sleepless night and with the in-laws out of the flat, my mother took the opportunity to flee Holland. After dressing Karen, and me she hastily packed a suitcase, took a few guilders from a bureau in the bedroom and we left Holland for the last time. From now on, it would be just the three of us.

Chapter 4

The Garden of England

...ten bob Tim...

Arriving back in England, with little more than the clothes on our backs, my mother knew there would be no room for us at Rose's place. She decided to make her way over to Dagenham, to see her sister Addy. It seemed to be my mother's only option at the time. There she found a warm welcome from her sister and a place to stay for a few days until she could get her bearings. She had not seen Addy since her own wedding and spent the next couple of days catching up on our comings and goings over the last three years. After a few days though, it was obvious to my mother that things were not sitting well with the rest of Addy's family.

It was then she decided to go see Rose and let her know how things had gone with Simon. Leaving Addy's place early that morning, we made our way over to Pitsea. Although Rose was sympathetic to my mother's predicament, she was still trying to come to grips with the death of her daughter Helen. Her home had only two bedrooms, and with her husband, young son Jim, and Granddad Regan all living under the same roof, there was little room.

Rose suggested that my mother make her way over to the Salvation Army; they would be able to look after our needs and find us a place to live. After a cup of tea or two, we took a slow walk into town, my mother pondering her next move. On the way, she recognized her brother Tim across the street. She had not seen him since her wedding, some three years ago. When she called out to him, he crossed the road and gave my mother a big hug, and for the first time we met our Uncle Tim.

He had not done well at school, and according to my mother, had left at age fourteen to help with the family finances. He was now a master pipe fitter, well dressed, single, and living off the top shelf. As we were close to the Tavern in Pitsea, he offered to buy my mother a drink and a bite to eat. It was a warm late August afternoon as we sat outside the pub having our lunch. My mother filled Tim in on her short disastrous marriage. The failed business venture with Reg and Nora; how they had buggered of to Canada, leaving Simon holding the bag; which did not surprise Tim. Then she explained how Simon had threatened to keep Karen in Holland and the beating she had taken when she had gone back to get her. Lending her a sympathetic ear, he inquired as to what her next move might be. My mother told Tim that she was off to the Salvation Army to see if they could set her up with some living accommodations and money for food. It was at this point, Tim realized how desperate things were for his sister. "I'll tell you what, Till, I've just returned from Kent, and the hop picking is just getting underway. Why not take yourself and the kids down there and make a few bob? There is little chance Simon will ever find you down there, if he ever decides to come looking for you. It won't cost you anything for rent. They supply you with a hut and who knows what might happen?"

To pick my mother's spirits up, Tim began to reminisce about the good times they had spent as kids in the hop fields. "Remember the fun we had Till, Mum would pull us out of school and take us all down to Kent on the train? Two extra weeks off school, away from the dirt and pollution of the East End, out into the clean fresh air in the country. Scrumped a bit of fresh fruit, pilfered a few fish, ride around on the hop wagon after we had finished our quota for the day. Remember "Jack Shit," the kid that got his nickname after he slipped in the pasture and sat down in a fresh cow-paddy and Mum's rabbit stew, it had to be the best!" Yes, they were good times, and as they sat there swapping stories; my mum recalled the time Jim needed to pee while on the train. "Dad got the pot out for him, and he did his business in it, when he had finished, dad opened the window to throw it out and the wind caught it and it all blew back in his face."

Before they knew it, it was two o'clock in the afternoon, closing time for the pub. Tim by now had managed to cheer my mother up and lift her spirits. She had accepted the idea of going hop picking down in Kent. However, she still needed to get a little seed money from the Salvation Army for train-fare and food. It was at that point Tim slipped her a ten bob note and told her to head for Tunbridge Wells. With a quick goodbye, he wished us well and was gone.

Ten shillings was more than enough for train fare, food for a few days and a pack of smokes for my mum. In high spirits now and with the thought of renewing some of her childhood memories, we were on our way. The Pitsea train station was just up the hill from the Tavern. With a ten bob note in her purse, me on one arm, suitcase on the other, and Karen in hot pursuit, we headed for the train. At the station, my mother purchased one and two half tickets to Tunbridge Wells.

A large crowd of people had gathered on the platform, most of them waiting for the Hop-Picker-Special. Making our way through the crowd, my mother found a place to sit and have a smoke. It wasn't long before she struck up a conversation with a young couple who had two children about the same age as Karen and me. The husband inquired as to which farm my mother was going to be working at. "I have no idea yet," she said, "I'm taking the train to Tunbridge Wells, where my mother used to go when we were kids. I plan on checking out the situation when I get there." He then informed my mother that she required a letter from the farm to confirm her employment and a booking for a hut in order to have a place to live, a point my mother and Tim had overlooked.

Thinking back on it now, my mother did recall the time when Aunt Alice had given her father a letter confirming employment at a hop farm when she had been unable to go one year. It was an anxious time for some Londoners, while their families waited on the postman to bring a letter verifying their employment at a hop farm. My mother now found herself in a bit of a quandary. The man, however, told her she could come with him and his family. They were going to a farm close to Tumbridge Wells. There was lots of work there and he could probably arrange something for her.

He introduced himself as Frank Collins, his wife Mary, and their two children David, and Dawn. He had worked at this particular farm for five seasons, the past two as a tallyman. He got on well with the bailiff, and was sure there would be no problem finding her a job and a place to live.

There was lots of chitchat and camaraderie among the pickers, as they caught up on all the gossip. Many, who had worked together in past years, had not seen one another since the last hop-picking season. Soon, there was the sound of a train whistle in the distance and a rowdy cheer went up. Pulling into the station, hissing steam and belching smoke the train ground slowly to a stop. The ear-piercing squeal of the brakes on steel wheels sent small children scurrying for the shelter of their parents.

Doors swung open revealing carriages full of families headed for the hop fields. A rush of bodies pushed forward, all looking for the few seats that would be available. My mother managed to find a place to sit and sat Karen and me on our old suitcase. Other kids sat on their parents knees or stood at the windows. Meeting Tim and convincing her that she should go hop picking had taken a load off my mothers mind. Although the sight of all these pickers on the train did make her a little anxious about her prospects of finding work in the hop fields. No matter what lay ahead for us now though, my mother was ready to turn the page on the last three years of our life.

With the sound of the porter's whistle and the shout of "All aboard!" doors slammed shut and with a wave of his flag, we were off. A sudden jolt reverberated down the length of the train as we pulled out of the station. Thick black smoke, puffed past the windows as we picked up speed. The clickerty clack, clickerty clack rhythm of the steel wheels on the rails, set off a singsong that went on for a couple of hours. Soon, pickers began to arrive at their various stations and before getting off, made tentative plans for end of season parties at various pubs back at home.

Sitting there, puffing on a cigarette and enjoying the ambience of the moment, my mother reflected back on the times she had spent with her family hop-picking, good times and bad. Grandparents were taken out of the polluted East End of London and into the country for some clean fresh air. Kids got an extra couple of weeks off school. Dads, if they could swing it, got a note from the doctor excusing them from their regular jobs so they could spend a week or two in the country. The few additional pounds at the end of the hop season would always come in handy for back to school clothes or a little extra coal for the winter. On the downside, if the weather was cold and wet, hops could be slippery and picking would not be easy. The hop bines were hard on the hands and the hours were long. Living conditions could be unpleasant, to say the least, depending on the farm. One toilet between ten to fifteen families made the aroma around the hedge groves a little unpleasant by the end of hop-picking season. A single water tap with limited washing facilities did not help with one's personal hygiene either. In hindsight though, as with most of life's experiences, they were always some good times, none the less.

As the train ambled along through the Kentish countryside, we watched with interest as farms, orchards and wheat fields passed by. Young children stared out of the windows, some seeing cows and sheep grazing in lush green fields for the first time. With the sun now sinking low over the meadows, the fall evenings were beginning to draw in. A rising mist began to paint the hedge groves in a pastel white haze. Amidst all the laughter, my mother had peace of mind about this move. It was a time to put the past behind her and make a new life for us in Kent, "The Garden of England."

Grapes grown in good soil under the right conditions make a fine wine. Hence, it is with hops, grown in the right environment make a great beer. In Kent, the hop is the king of crops, with much of the domestic economy of Kent centered on it. The process starts early in the year, with men on six-foot high stilts, stringing the poles Once the young vines started to grow, farms hire local women to twist the young shoots onto the string. When the hops are in full bloom and ready for picking, its time for the hoards of Londoners to descend on the fields of Kent for the annual madness known as *"Hop picking time."*

Pulling into Tunbridge Wells, we joined the flood of pickers getting off the train, my mother staying close to Frank and his family. Passing through the station, and out onto the roadway, there were three old lorries waiting to haul pickers to their various farms. One of the drivers called out to Frank

"Over here mate!" There was a short conversation with the driver on my mother's behalf, and then we were loaded onto the back of a lorry and taken about two miles down the road to our farm.

Greeted by the bailiff, pickers were given their marching orders for Monday morning. The farm whistle would blow at six; the lorry will arrive at six thirty and leave the huts for the field at seven sharp. Miss it, and pickers would find themselves walking to work." With the hut numbers assigned, families began to move in. Due to the fact my mother had no letter of employment and the huts were all booked, the bailiff gave us one of the old barns to stay in. The barn used mostly for the storage of grain and hay, had what seem to be a small living area off to one corner. Table and chairs, an iron bedstead with a straw mattress were soon rustled up. Frank's wife got a hearty rabbit stew on the go and invited us for dinner. Later that evening, a group of gypsies pulled into the field next to the huts. They too had come for the hop-picking season. Gypsies, apart from picking hops, would make a little extra money on the side selling their wares; weaved baskets, cloths pegs and homemade medicinal remedies for whatever ails the body. The men would also make a little extra cash snaring rabbits and selling them to the pickers. Many of the Londoners and the gypsies knew each other from years past and spent most of the evening catching up on the latest gossip. For my mother, it had been a long exhausting day, so she thanked Mary for dinner and we took our leave. Returning to the barn, she made up our bed with borrowed blankets and we retired for the night.

At six o'clock, the farm whistle blew and soon after, there was a knock at the barn door. Mary had been up early that morning; she had a large pot of porridge on the go and invited us to join them. "Come on kids, get stuck into this," she said. "It'll stick to ya ribs all day and Tilly don't worry about lunch; I've packed a few extra sandwiches." My mother thanked her for her generosity, promising to repay her sometime. "Ah! Go on Tilly, what are friends for," she chuckled.

At six thirty, the lorry arrived and the men began to help load the women and children onto the back. It was a damp foggy, morning and when we arrived at the field, the dew hung heavy on the bines. Here, pickers were given their bins and directed to their rows. My mother, eager to get started, pulled her first bine and got a cold shower for her effort. It didn't take long for her to get down to work. Early training from her mother had taught her well and she began to scratch the hops into her bin like a pro.

With the shyness of youth, my sister and I started to mingle with some of the other kids. Exploring around the field, we came across some women handing out sandwiches and tea. One of the women offered me a sandwich and taking it, I ran back to my mum to tell her what was happening. My mother, under the impression that Mary had given me the sandwich, went on picking. It was not until the Salvation Army Ladies got down to her end of the field did she realized what was going on. "The angels of lunchtime had arrived," as my mother put it. She too had a sandwich and a cup of tea. That took care of our lunch for the day.

By noon, the fog had burned off, and it turned into a sunny afternoon. Frank stopped by to check on my mother and see how she was doing. He mentioned that she could get an advance on her pay if she needed some money. She told him that five shillings would help her out until the end of the week. At four-thirty the sound of "Pull no more bines!" was heard and my mother's first day in the hop-field ended. That evening, we walked into the village to pick up some groceries and sweets.

The first week of picking had gone well, and for the first time in a long while, my mother felt good about her situation. She had made a few bob, as she could really scratch those hops off the vine. Karen and I were happy and we had a roof over our heads. Friday afternoon, we went into the village where my mother bought new blankets, a tablecloth and a few new dishes. These were items she had borrowed from friends and needed to return. For dinner that night, my mother laid out the tablecloth and set the table with the new dishes and cutlery. Taking a large chunk of cheese she had purchased at the store, she proceeded to melt it in a pot along with some milk and margarine. After toasting the bread, she poured the mixture over the bread and topped it off with a couple of slices of tomato. "*Welsh Rarebit,*" became one of our favourite meals at teatime. Bedtime was a real pleasure too, with our new blankets and pillows.

The following week, my mother purchased a small primus stove, making it easier for us to have a cup of tea in the mornings. Although things were going well for her at the present, my mother was concerned about what would happen to us in a few more weeks, when hop picking would be finished. A few of the folks she worked with were from the London area and tried to convince her to go back there. Things were starting to pick up now after the war and there was employment for anyone who wanted to work. Some of the jobs even offered two weeks paid holiday, sending Londoners on vacation to the seaside or holiday camp rather than picking hops. Even so, having grown up in the East End of London, my mother knew what the realities of life would be for a single parent with two small children growing up in the city. The slum living conditions and the polluted air affected people's health. When kids had colds, they would often cough up black sooty sputum. My mother had walked the country lanes around the hop fields, seen little cottages with their flower gardens and felt the clean fresh air of Kent. This was the kind of place she desired to raise her family. The pace of life was slower and less complicated. Besides, a job prospect had come up in the form of an ad placed on a bulletin board in the village. A farm was advertising for someone to cook, clean and look after two farmhands, plus the landlady. Taking the note off the board, my mother filed it in her purse for future reference. This could be her opportunity to get back to a cooking career. A profession she had apprenticed at in London, before the war broke out and she had gone to work in a munitions factory.

Returning home to the huts one afternoon after work, the pickers found a gang of didicoys had moved in just down the road from the hoppers compound. Didicoys are scam-artists, prone to making a dishonest living. Their inbred looks, sneering lingo, long greasy hair and dishevelled clothing, made them a menacing sight to see. The ramshackle caravans and covered carts were an unwelcome sight to see; a drab contrast to the fine-looking gypsy caravans. It was not good news to have them camped anywhere near the compound, as they would steal your belongings just as soon as look at them.

The first few days they kept to themselves; then they started to come over and mingle with the men. Pickers knew this was just a ploy to scope out the compound to see if there were any easy pickings. For a time, the men engaged them in conversation just to keep the peace, but their tactics fooled no one. Most of the pickers felt that the huts and their belonging would not be safe if left alone all day. It was decided that some of the men would wander back now and then just to keep an eye on the huts. It worked well for the first few days, until one of the men let his guard down. He had returned to the huts to check things out, and then lay down to have a nap. It was while he slept that the didicoys struck.

Returning home that evening after a long day in the field, my mother found that some one had entered our barn. The new blankets along with the bedstead, tablecloth and primus stove were all missing. She had no doubt as to who had been in the barn, or where her belongings had gone. Didicoys! They had obviously done their homework and targeted what they thought was the weakest link in the encampment, a big mistake on their part.

My mother appealed for a few of the men to come with her to the didicoys' camp and see if they could help her find her things. None of the men was willing or wanted to confront these no-good drifters, telling my mother it was best for her to let it go. "You have no proof, Tilly," said Frank, "and things could get ugly." Having none of it, my mother plucked up her nerve, and marched right across the road and into the midst of their camp. Noticing what look like her bedstead leaning against one of the wagon, she demanded the return of her belongings. Met with an onslaught of verbal abuse, my mother told them she was going into the village to report the theft of her property, if it was not back in her barn by the time she got back, she would lay charges against the lot of them. "Hey lady, we ain't got none of your shat," snarled one of them. "Ya got a bloody cheek comin over ear accusing folks of pinching ya stuff," grunted another. "Ya best foock off now before I sets the dag's on ya," "Yeh, well the same to you mate with brass knobs on."

These were my mother's final words, and with that, she left and headed for the village. Returning home a short time later, she found all our belongings back in the barn. The didicoys told the other pickers they thought the barn had been deserted. "I don't know Tilly," said Frank. "That took a lot of pluck. I don't think I could have gone over there if that had been my stuff." By now, my mother had had enough of pickers, pikey's and didicoys. It was late, she was tired, hungry, and all she wanted to do was have something to eat, and get to bed.

The next morning, after the ordeal with the didicoys, she thought long and hard about the cook-domestic job and decided she would go into the village after work and look into it. Finishing our breakfast, we went out to catch the lorry. After the theft, pickers agreed that someone would remain in the compound fulltime while the didicoys were camped across the road. It was not long either until the didicoys caught onto the Sally Ann tea women. They began hanging around the hop field during the day for a free cup of tea and sandwich.

Later that day, after we had finished lunch and my mother had gone back to picking for the afternoon, my sister and I found a frog. This was the first time either of us had seen one. As it hopped around the field trying to make its escape, a crowd of kids gathered on behind, giving the frog a poke whenever it stopped. Hopping closer and closer to the river, it finally reached the bank and made its big escape. Taking one enormous leap, it splashed into the river, and began its swim to freedom.

Having no understanding of water or its consequences,

I took my own long leap into the river after the frog. Once in the water, I found myself out of my depth, chocking and struggling to breathe. My mother, hearing the screams and yells from the kids, instinctively responded, without a second thought, she ran across the field and jumped into the river after me. Unable to swim herself, she grabbed me by my hair and did her best to keep my head out of the water. Following right behind my mother, two other men dove into the river, helping drag us both ashore. Sitting on the riverbank, choking and still in shock, my mother finally pulled herself together and made her way over to thank the two men who had helped pull us out of the river. With eyes still full of tears and river water, she approached them and began to express her gratitude. Realizing that as she did, she was coming face to face with two of the didicoys she had accused of stealing our belongings from the barn. "Don't mention it lady," said one. "All in a day's work." said the other with a grin.

Two days later, I came down with dysentery, a fact that did not surprise the doctor, as the river was used as a dump for the outhouse buckets. The near drowning would be the end of my mother's hop picking days. Under the pretence of taking me to the doctor again, she went into the village the phoned after the domestic job at Hill Side Farm. After a short conversation with the landlady, they set a time and date, for an interview the following Monday.

Weekends at the hop fields were a time for the women to take a break from the fields and catch up with their washing and cleaning. The men's job was to clean the outhouses, look for firewood and pack in some water. Saturday night would find most of the pickers down at one of the local pubs. For the men, this was a time to let off a little steam. For the women, it was a chance to have a much-earned break from the hop field, and the cares of the family. They also needed to keep a tight fist on the purse strings, as they did most of the picking and knew how hard the money was to come by. Many of the local pubs did not care to have the pickers business. They tried to put them off by placing signs in the window indicating they were not welcome. These signs, directed mostly at the didicoy element, as they caused many of the problems on a Saturday night. Other pubs would have two separate sides; one for pickers, with all the old furnishings and glasses, the other side was for the locals, with all their better-quality fixtures and glasses.

Not all pickers would spend their hard-earned money on a Saturday night at the local boozer. Many would pass the time in the evening around the campfire with their families; have a little singsong, swap a few stories and reflect on what they would do with their hop-picking money. After dinner on Saturday nights, my mother would take us for a walk into the village; here she would pick herself up her favourite, milk stout and lemonade, and crisps for Karen and me. We would then return to the compound and join in with the group around the fire.

Sunday was a time to take it easy. Children entertained themselves on a tree swing or a made-up seesaw. Men would use the time nursing hangovers, taking a nap, or playing cards. The women needed to wash clothes, bath the kids, and prepare an evening meal. Following dinner on a Sunday evening, the Salvation Army would come by and do a church service with hymns, gospel readings and a short message. Following the service, there was a time of fellowship with sandwiches, and hot drinks. It was a much-appreciated break for the women, a time for them to sit back, relax, and have someone else makes the tea.

Monday morning, my mother excused herself from work. She had arranged a ten o'clock appointment with Mrs. Hills of Hill Side Farm. They were to meet at a small teashop in the village. Mrs Hills was a middle-aged woman who had never been married. She had inherited the farm from her parents, and depended on hired help to run it. Mrs. Hills explained to my mother that she would be responsible for cooking and cleaning for her and two farm hands. She would have a prepared menu to work from and the use of a donkey and cart to get back and forth to the village for groceries. My mother's work hours were Monday to Friday, six to six with weekends off. Mrs. Hills would have one of her men pick us up on Friday, giving my mother a chance to settle in on the weekend.

Chapter 5

Hillside Farm

"Goin' to the derby, lookin' very smart,
Doin' all the journey in me donkey cart."
Stanley Holloway

It was early Friday afternoon when we arrived at Hillside Farm. Located about five miles from the hop fields and nestled in the southwest corner of Kent. Mainly a grain-growing farm, it also had a small herd of dairy cows. Mrs. Hills, the landlady, a rather portly looking woman was in her garden working; here she grew most of her own vegetables. Beyond the garden was an old apple orchard; where she kept a large flock of free-range chickens for egg production. Placing a few carrots, along with some potatoes she had been harvesting into her basket, she slowly stood up, as if dealing with a touch of lumbago, and came over to greet us. "Lovely day isn't it," she said with a half-hearted smile, as she introduced herself to Karen and me. Leading us down the garden path, we entered the back door of the farmhouse into the scullery. Placing the basket of produce into a large stone sink, she asked Roy, the farm hand, to take our suitcase to the upstairs bedroom. Removing her wellies and pinafore and hanging up her rather outsized straw bonnet, Mrs. Hills excused herself to go wash-up, telling my mother to have a look around the place.

The scullery had a slate-floor and up against an outside wall was a large coal fired copper for doing the laundry. Attached to the stone sink was an old-fashioned cast iron water pump. The sink itself was used mostly for the cleaning and preparation of vegetables. Behind the sink, a small bay window overlooking the garden, in the alcove were a number of potted plants in various stages of survival. A low oak beam ceiling ran from the scullery on into the kitchen-dinning area. Set back in a stone inglenook was a large black cast-iron cook-stove with a side oven; two flatirons sat on the back of the stove ready for ironing. Dominating the room was a very large, well-worn wooden table. The chairs too, showed their age and had stiff straight backs that were very uncomfortable to sit on. The table, my mother soon found out, also doubled as a workbench when the men needed to make repairs to the horse harness.

Roy returned a few minutes later and started explaining to my mother about the daily operations of the farm. Tony the other farmhand and Roy were up at five-thirty to do the morning milk. They came back to the house around seven for breakfast. The afternoon milking was normally finished around six; this is when they would have their dinner. Depending on the workload and the chores at hand, it was possible they would need a packed lunch some days. Right now, they were bringing in the last of the stooks for thrashing. This meant they would be back and forth between the field and the farmhouse for the next few days and would have their lunch at the house. As soon as the ploughing started, they would need a packed lunch.

After washing up, Mrs. Hills returned and asked Roy to take Karen and me outside for a tour of the farm while she showed my mother around the house and explained some of her duties. The vegetables, milk and eggs from the farm were at my mother's disposal for any of her cooking needs. We would eat in the kitchen with the men, while Mrs. Hills would have her meals served in her private sitting room. Eggs had to be collected once a day, cleaned and taken to town twice a week, where my mother would exchange them for credit at the local grocery store. After listing off my mother's duties, Mrs. Hills told her that she would be on a two-week probation period. If she was satisfied with her work and the men had no complaints with her cooking, the job would be hers.

Outside, Tony introduced us to the old farm dog, "Lucky."

He was born a runt of the litter to a boarder collie on one of the neighbouring sheep farms. Tony picked the pup up some eight years ago and taught him how to herd the cows. As we entered the milking shed, three large skittish cats made a dash for the hayloft. According to Tony, the only time they were friendly was at milking time when they got a dish of fresh milk. In another barn, Roy was in the process of harnessing one of the large, chestnut-coloured carthorses with all its leather and brass finery. Hillside Farm had not yet switch to tractors and were still using horses for most of their farming needs. Roy offered to take us for a ride on the back of this gentle giant. Karen and I shook our heads rapidly, conveying the message to Roy of, "no thanks!"

One other means of transportation on the farm was this funny-looking little horse with long ears, short legs and a big head. Roy explained to us that it was a donkey, and her name was Primrose. At one time, in her youth, she had been a champion racer at the Donkey Derby held at the town fête each year. However, one year she had absolutely refused to leave the starting line. An oddity discovered a few days later would put an end to her derby days forever.

This donkey was not a bit like the fine-looking horse Tony was grooming. Because she was such an odd-looking animal and she made us laugh, Karen and I decided to call her Funny-Face. Roy suggested that we might use the donkey and cart to go into the village for shopping. The little red cart had yellow spoke wheels with rubber rims, emblazoned on either side was the name, *"Hillside Farm."*

A little while later, Mrs. Hills and my mother joined us outside and Mrs. Hills confirmed that this would indeed be our means of transportation to and from the village. Mrs. Hills suggested Roy give my mother some direction on how to hook up the cart, and point out a few of the peculiarities the donkey had. After showing my mother the basics on how to hook up the wagon, Roy asked us to jump aboard. The first little quirk we found out was that Funny-Face never wanted to leave the farmyard. One had to physically lead her out to the road and point her in the direction of the village. Nervously we sat in the back with our mum as Roy walked Funny-Face out to the road. Hopping aboard, he gave the reins a gentle slap and we were off down the road at a leisurely pace. It was not to long before we would learn about another quirk that Funny-Face had. Remember the oddity that had ended her donkey-derby-days. Well coming to a sudden stop in the middle of the road, Funny-Face refused to go any further; Roy explained to us what the problem was. If there were anything in the road, such as a leaf or a twig, the donkey would come to a sudden stop and wait until someone removed it. Once the object was removed, she would then carry on again. Warming up to the adventure, Karen and I took turns jumping on and off the wagon to remove the offending items. This was very amusing to my sister and me and with fall close at hand, there was no shortage of leaves on the road.

Friday nights, after the evening milk, the men were accustomed to going into the village for a bite to eat. As it was Friday, Tony invited us to join them. After finishing the evening chores, we were back in the cart and off down the road to town for a fish and chip supper. Returning home, my mother took stock of the pantry, as she planned to do some shopping on Saturday. While busying herself with a shopping list, Mrs. Hills popped in to give her some instructions on a special fare she was preparing. At the back of the pantry, sitting on a stone shelf covered with a cloth, was a large round cheese, the size of a small car tire. In the center was a hole, about one inch in diameter. Next to the cheese was a bottle of port. My mother's job was to top up the hole in the cheese with the port when it was getting low. The job of keeping an eye on the level of the port, my mum passed on to Karen and me. Each day, we would check the cheese and let her know if the port in the hole was getting low.

Friday had been a full and exciting day for us and we retired to bed early that evening. Our room in the attic with its low gentle slopping walls and ceiling gave it a cave-like appearance. A large dormer to one side of the room offered us a full view of the farmyard. That night, we slept in a warm feather bed, unlike the straw-filled mattress back at the hop-pickers barn. In the morning, we woke early to an array of barnyard prattle. The sound of cows, chickens and horses filled the space outside our window. However, a peculiar hee-haw sound seemed rather strange to us. Looking out of the window, we saw that it was Funny-Face, braying for her breakfast.

The day had started early for men, Tony and Roy had been up since five thirty to do the morning milk. My mother also rose early, as she wanted to get breakfast on the go for the men. She also needed help hooking up the cart so she could go into the village to shop. This morning would be our first jaunt into the village with the donkey and cart by ourselves. Returning from the hen house, my mother took a dozen large brown golden-yoked eggs, cracked them into a bowl and made scrambled eggs. Eager to get going, Karen and I finished our breakfast and went outside to wait for our mum. Sitting on an old farm wagon, we watched the men bridle up two of the large horses. They were going to the blacksmiths this day to be re-shod. Shortly our mother joined us outside, while Roy helped her hitched up the cart, my sister and I waited out by the road. Leading Funny-Face out of the farmyard, my mother pointed her in the direction of the village and we all jumped aboard the cart. With a flick of the reins and a "giddy-up," we were off down the road. If my mother had any doubts about the donkey and cart, she did not let it show. This would be the first of many adventures into the village.

With another full day on the farm over with, we retired to bed early that evening. During the middle of the night, we were startled by a loud thumping noise echoing across the farmyard. Lying there in the dark, my mother tried to make some sense of where the noise was coming from. Climbing out of bed, she crept slowly over to the window, followed close behind by my sister and me. Staring out the window into the foggy night, the sound seemed to be coming from the direction of the stables. Crouching down on the floor, we watched and waited. Something was thumping on the stable door. Soon it began to wobble and splinter; finally, the door came off its hinge. It was clear to us by now as the horses made their escape that they had kicked down the barn door. By the time the men finally made it out to the yard, the horses had made their escape into the night.

In the morning, Roy told my mother this had happened once before after the horses had been re-shod. "We're not quite sure if they were unhappy with the new shoes, or just wanted to try them out." Either way, he told my mother to keep Karen and me in the house, until they had rounded up the horses.

By now, it was early October. With the harvest in and most of the ploughing done, life on the farm began to settle into a slower pace. Tony mention to my mother that it was

Roy's fiftieth birthday in a few days. He would like to have a small party for him and wondered if it was possible for my mother to bake him a cake. Because of the wartime rations, some baking needs were still in limited supply. My mother told Tony it would not be any bother, she would work it into the food budget. The birthday soon rolled around and plans made to have the party after the men had finished the evening milk on Saturday. My mother hitched up Funny-Face to the wagon that morning and we went into the village to pick up the groceries. One of Roy's favourite meals was Toad in the Hole.

In the village, she called in at the local butcher shop and bought fresh sausages. Her next stop was the local grocery store where she traded the eggs and picked up her groceries and a small gift of some socks for Roy. Passing the local pub on our way home, my mother noticed Tony and Roy sitting outside having an afternoon birthday beer. Seeing my mother pass by, they called us over to join them. Ordering her favourite, milk stout, my sister and I had a lemonade and bag of crisps each. While sitting there enjoying a few laughs, it just so happened that Mrs. Hills drove by. My mother, giving her a friendly wave, had her gesture returned with a pretentious look. The men did not attach too much significance to it, waving it off as just an upper class snub; my mother however, felt offended and took it personally.

At two o'clock, closing time, the men decided they would load their bicycles into the cart and ride back home with us. Rolling into the farm in a jovial mood, my mother took the groceries into the house while the men unhooked Funny Face. Tony and Roy then retired for an afternoon nap before doing the evening milk, Tony, confirming with my mother that they would have the cake after all the chores were done for the day.

Later that afternoon while my mum and Karen busied themselves mixing up the cake, Mrs. Hills came into the kitchen. Obviously bothered somewhat, she paced up and down the kitchen a few times, studying what the two of them were up to. When she finally spoke, she informed my mother she was not happy with her socializing with the farm hands in public and would prefer that it did not happen again. Also, as it was Saturday, my mother's day off, the donkey and cart were not a means of transportation for her and the men to use for personal jaunts. My mother, although annoyed by her comments, calmed herself and held her tongue. Mrs. Hills then inquired as to what she was making. My mother explained that it was Roy's fiftieth and she was baking him a cake to celebrate his birthday. Mrs. Hills told my mother she could stop what she was doing right now, "You were not hired to bake birthday cakes for the men," she said in an ill-tempered tone. Then, with rationing in effect, she inquired as to how my mother had managed to get the ingredients to make a cake. My mother explained to her that she had worked it into the food budget and there had been no extra cost involved. Mrs. Hills then advised my mother that she would be docking a half-crown from her pay packet next week to cover the extra expenses. At that point, my mother had heard enough. Fortified by a couple of milk stouts, she reminded Mrs. Hills that Saturday was indeed her day off and she would in fact, do as she pleased on her days off. If that meant having a drink with the men or baking a cake, then so be it. The trip into the village she explained had not been a personal jaunt. She had taken eggs into the grocery shop for resale. She then explained to Mrs. Hills that she had promised the cake for Roy's birthday and she was bloody well going to finish it. Mrs. Hills, not waiting for my mother to finish, stomped out of the kitchen.

Although agitated by the haughty attitude of Mrs. Hills, my mother began to have second thoughts about what she had just said. After all, Mrs. Hills was the landlady. Putting the disagreement behind her for the time being, my mum finished the cake and put it in the oven. My sister and I licked out the mixing bowl. Mrs. Hills returned a short time later and told my mother that she was dismissing her from her duties, and she was to be out of the house by Monday.

Feeling a little numb, my mother now realized she had made a big mistake. With less than a month of employment at the farm she should have been a little more subservient, a quality that somehow seem to escape my mothers Cockney Irish make-up. She enjoyed her job on the farm; she knew Karen and I were happy living there too. "What ever was to become of us now?" she thought. Winter was setting in. Where were we to go? However, no matter how hard she tried, she could not bring herself to go, make amends, and maybe get her job back.

Setting it all behind her for the time being, she prepared the Yorkshire pudding mix for Toad in the Hole, and put it in the oven. She then iced the cake and wrapped up the present while Karen and I laid-up the table. As the men came into the scullery to wash-up, she placed the cake in the centre of the table along with the present, much to Roy's surprise.

After dinner, my mother knew she had to let the men know she was leaving. For that reason, she recounted the events of the afternoon that had led up to the firing. Disappointed by the situation, the men could not help thinking their conduct could have been part of the problem, especially the fiddle with the rations to bake a birthday cake.

To change the mood, my mother decided that a drink might cheer them all up. With that intention, she went into the pantry and brought out the bottle of port. Taking three cups from the cupboard, she poured a shot of port for each of them and they drank to one another's good health. Soon the conversations turned to the more serious side of things. What was my mother going to do? Where were we going to go? Tony suggested that he had a friend by the name of Jim Buller who lived near Charing. He always knew of a few cheap rental properties and might be able to help her out with a place to live. Tony said he would go into the village on Sunday and give Jim a ring at his local watering hole.

Sunday morning, my mother made up a picnic lunch. Ignoring Mrs. Hill's remarks, she hitched up the donkey and cart and for the last time we spent a day out in the country. After threading our way around the maze of lanes that surrounded the farm, we returned home late that afternoon. At suppertime, Tony told my mother that he had been in contact with his friend Jim at Charing. He did have a caravan for rent that might interest her. It was a little way out of Charing, but on a bus route. He would meet us at Monkery Bottom, Monday afternoon around two o'clock.

Tony suggested that he take us into town in the morning and make sure we got on the right bus to Maidstone. There we would need to transfer to the Canterbury bus. Getting off at the top of Charing Hill, it would be about a one-mile walk down the Faversham road to Monkery Bottom.

In the morning, my mother packed our belongings in our old suitcase and we went downstairs for breakfast with the men. Mrs. Hills came in with my mother's final pay packet, a half-crown short and laid it on the table. She left with out any discussion. After we had eaten, Tony took our suitcase out to the car. My mother taking one last look around observed the empty port bottle sitting on the counter. In one final act of rebellion, she took a bottle of malt vinegar from the cupboard, went into the pantry, uncovered the cheese and filled the hole with the vinegar.

Rose   Nora   Addy   Tim   Tilly

Adelaide   Tim

Tim   Tilly   Rose   Nora   Nelly
Mother

Tim   Nora   Mother   Nelly   Tilly

John and Jim - Two wild and crazy guys.

Nelly
Grand Ma and Grand Pa
Joan & Pat

Tim, Simon, Tilly and Tim Regan, Sr.

John's Christning, Karen, Tilly.

Simon, circa 1935

Mum, Dad, Karen and John, outside our railcar in Holland.

Tilly and hospital co-workers.

Karen and John
School days in Charing.

Pevington Farm.
John and Mum, Sylvia, Karen, Micheal, and Norman.

Aunt Margreat, Uncle Alan, Mum, Marie and Tony.

Lenham Sanatorium
Christmas Party
Circa 1952

The best dance of the evening.

Serving lunch, T.B. Sanatorium Lenham.

John and Karen, Charing Hill. 1951

Hothfield Christmas Party. Circa 1955

Reuion 2005
Robin Murrell, Steve Mathews, Micheal Teesdale (Taffy) John Roders

Chapter 6

Monkery Bottom

when I say a home, I mean it was just a derelict old bus, but it was home to us

The fall of 1950 would find us living in a small dirt lay-by along the Faversham road known as Monkery Bottom. This is where Tony, the farmhand from Hillside Farm, had directed my mother to go. She was to meet a friend of his by the name of Jim Buller, who might have a small caravan for us to rent.

We left Hillside Farm Monday morning, our old suitcase filled with all that we owned. Tony took us into Tumbridge Wells where we caught a bus to Maidstone; there we transferred to the Canterbury bus. Leaving Maidstone my mother enquired of the bus conductor if he could point out where the Faversham and Canterbury roads met, so that we might be able to find our way to Monkery Bottom. He told my mum that the stop she needed was at the top of Charing Hill. He would let her know when it was time for us to get off. As we approached our destination, the bus pulled to the curb and the conductor directed my mother towards the Faversham road. "Monkery Bottoms down that road luv, about a mile past the Pub, ya can't miss it." My mother thanked him, and we were on our way.

It was a chilly, October afternoon as the three of us made our way down the road for about a mile, arriving at a small dirt lay-by occupied by a gypsy family. With a campfire burning, gypsy horses grazing the hedgerows, and the sunlight glinting off their brightly painted wagon, made for a romantic picture. Looking around though, my mother saw nothing that resembled a caravan, just an old derelict bus parked off to one side. Questioned by one of the gypos as to her business there, my mother told him she was there to meet a Jim Buller to see about renting a caravan. "Do you know of him?" my mother enquired. "Jim Buller, Aye! no's him well, he'll probably wanna stick ya with that there ramshackled old bus. Ah don't think ya wanna be a rentin that tho. Had a few old tramps spend a night or two in it, and some yobo's have smashed out a few of the windows, ma self, I wouldn't livin it rent free." Thinking she might have the wrong location, my mother questioned him as to whether this was Monkery Bottom. "Yeh, luv, this be it, spend most our winters here each year, but that old bus, she ain't bin lived in for the last two, running alive with mice and crap, eh! Care for a cup a tea whiles ya waitin' Miss?"

Introducing himself as Steve and his wife, Jill, he threw a handful of tealeaves into a large smoke-blackened pot hanging on a wooden trivet over the fire and invited us to sit down. My mother introduced herself as Tilly and my sister and me as Karen and John, "Ah, nice ta meet ya."

As my mum sat chatting and drinking tea into the late afternoon, the fall air began to chill us. With no sign of Mr. Buller, she started to become quite anxious as to what she should do. She told Steve, if that bus was the rental, she was probably not interested and if we left right now, we could still make it back to Ashford and check in with the Salvation Army for the night. A thought my mother did not relish. Thanking Steve and Jill for the tea, we got up and began walking towards the road, just as an old Morris van rolled into the enclosure. Exiting the vehicle was a rather rough looking middle-aged fellow with a stubby-grey-beard; a dog-end stuck out the corner of his mouth. His long greasy hair hung out from under a ragged looking cheese-cutter hat. The tattered tweed jacket that he wore was threadbare at the elbows. A cord tied around the waist held up his trousers, the cuffs of which he had tucked inside his old turned-down Wellington boots. "Eh Tilly!" he called out to my mother in a raspy tone, "I'm Jim, Tony's friend." Making his way toward us now, he commented, "I'm here ta rent ya that there bus." "Ya gota be jokin!" hollered Steve. Jim, turning in Steve's direction, shook his finger at him and growled "Shut ya mouth mate, or I'll have you, ya misses and that ol-cart outer here faster than beer turns ta piss." Jill, in a mood of cheeky defiance asked, "How much ya gonna rush her for that shit-hole?" Giving her a blinding look, Jim ignored the comment and took us over to the bus. As we approached, it was obvious that this ancient means of transport had been sitting there for some time, wheels missing, windows cracked and broken, and a spindly looking tree growing out of the engine compartment. There was more rust on that old corpse of a bus than paint. A large metal barrel by the door had a makeshift gutter coming off the roof for collecting rainwater. Set back in the trees was an old wooden shed, that was our outhouse.

Kicking the weeds aside from the front entrance and giving the corroded door a good boot, Jim went inside, "Come on in, Tilly," he said, beckoning to my mother. Standing by the bus door there seemed to be an unpleasant odour emanating from within. Once inside though, it was obvious that the smell was coming from a combination of mice, mould and charred wood left in the stove and the fact that Mr. Buller could sorely use a bath. Soot from the old woodstove covered the sparse furnishings, and mice droppings littered the floor. Broken windows, patched with cardboard had blown in, leaving the curtains hanging in tatters and covered in rust stains and cobwebs. "A little spit and polish it'll look like new. Five bob a week, what ya say Tilly?" With not a lot of options left and trying to look on the bright side of things, my mother took it. She must have seen some potential in the place, no doubt reflecting back on the home she had made in an old railcar not so long ago. Opening her purse, she handed him the five shillings. He told her he would be by each Saturday morning for the rent, and if she could be there then, he would appreciate it. Then with a tip of his hat, he bade us a courteous goodnight and was gone.

After he left, my mother sunk into one of the old wooden chair, and in a mood of hopeless exhaustion, began to sob uncontrollably. My sister and I were unable to console her. An unexpected knock at the door brought her quickly back to her senses. Looking through the mildew-stained glass of the buses front entrance, she could see that it was Jill standing there. Pulling herself together, my mother pushed the door opened. "What's a matter, luv?" asked Jill. "We can hear ya howling all the way out here. Come! Have another cup of tea and a fag and tell us all about it, hon."

After tea, a good chat, and a few more tears, my mother borrowed a bucket and broom and a bar of lye soap from Jill and set about cleaning house. Her first order of business was to throw out the old rotting mattress. Taffy, the old woodcutter from down the road had heard of my mother's plight through Steve. He brought us a sack of firewood, and offered to get a fire going. After placing a bucket of water on the stove, my mother took the old table and chairs outside, then gave the inside of the bus a good sweep. It was not long before things began to warm up. When the bucket of hot water was ready, she placed a couple of old pots and some dishes in the sink to soak and gave the kitchen area a good scrub. Placing another bucket of water on the stove to boil, she began to replace as much of the old cardboard as possible to keep out the cold. With another bucket of water, she cleaned the table, chairs and the bedstead. After a couple more buckets of hot soapy water sloshed over the floor and scrubbed with the broom, she felt the place was clean enough to call it a night. Bringing the table and chairs back inside the bus, she gave the kettle a good scrub and put it on the stove for tea. Jill brought over a candle, a loaf of bread, and some jam and soon, tea and doorstep sized sandwiches were on the table ready to fill the holes in our bellies. The friendship with Steve and Jill would last throughout the winter.

After tea, my mother made up the bed with a couple of old blankets laid out on the bedstead. With our clothes still on, we climbed into bed, my mum in the middle. She then pulled her old coat over top of the blanket for a little extra warmth. Blowing out the candle, we cuddled up close to her and slept the first night in the old bus. We would call Monkery Bottom and this old bus home for the duration of the winter and on into spring.

In the morning, the bus was a damp and chilly place to be. Throughout the night, unbeknownst to my sister and me, our mother had spent most of the night swatting mice as they ran over our bed. When my mother got out of bed and went to put on her shoes, she found a mouse in the toe of one of them. This set her off with a few choice words as she tried in vain to clobber it with her shoe. While my sister and I lay in bed quite amused by the episode, our mother got the fire going and put the kettle on for a pot of tea, and more bread and strawberry jam sandwiches.

At that time, Robinson's Jams came with a little Golly-black-boy-sticker just inside the lid. There was always a fight between my sister and me, as to who would get the Golly. A fight that was always settled by our mother. At the time, you could collect them, stick them on a card and when it was full, you could trade it in for a free jar of jam, a prize that for some reason had always eluded my mother. Misfortune would always some-how befall the card and we would have to start over again. One time, I remembered the card was just about full and my mother was counting on the free jar of jam. During the night, the card had fallen to the floor, the scent of the jam had attracted mice and they chewed the card to shreds, much to my mother's chagrin.

After breakfast, my mother went about fixing holes in the walls and floor where it was obvious mice were getting in. Muttering all the while, as she crammed rags into holes and placed bricks in front of them, bricks obviously used before for the same purpose. Finishing-up the holes, she now turned her attention to Karen and me. "Come on kids, get out of that bed!" she hollered, "It's time to go to town and get some money; buy some new clothes, food, and maybe some sweets." For all Karen and I knew, money could have been growing on trees, all we heard was sweets, and we were out of bed in a flash. A quick slap and dash with the flannel and we were on our way up the road to Charing to catch a bus into Ashford.

In town, my mother headed straight for the Social Assistance Office, where she hoped to plead her case and pick up some welfare money to tide her over until she could find some form of employment. Here, she was introduced to a Mrs. Housdan, a very gracious, courteous, and professional woman. After taking down my mother's particulars, and giving a sympathetic ear to her plight, she turned her attention to my sister Karen and me. We were not in school. A detail my mother had overlooked due to the fact she was still trying to come to grips with her broken marriage and the demands of putting a roof over our heads. My sister had turned five that summer and by rights, she should have been in school. If my mother were to go to work, it would be easier for her if I, young as I was, were in school too. She advanced my mother enough money for school uniforms, food and rent for the next week. Mrs. Housdan also set in motion paperwork for my mother to collect alimony from my father if at any time he were ever to return to England and work. She also agreed to pay us a visit as soon as the schooling was in place.

Leaving Mrs. Housdan's office that morning was the first time I had seen any real joy on my mother's face in a while. Our first stop was a café, where we tucked into a pot of tea, cheese rolls and for a treat, ice cream for my sister and me. Then it was onto Marks & Spencer's for school uniforms; cap and blazer, shirt and tie, socks and shoes, for both my sister and me. We had never been so well off. Our next stop would be the Salvation Army thrift shop, where my mother picked up curtains, a small carpet, some dishes, bed clothes, candles, a large can of white wash paint and a couple of mousetraps. By now, we were well loaded down and it was time to head home.

Arriving back at Monkery Bottom, the neighbours thought we had won the Foot Ball Pools. While our mum got tea on the table, my sister and I played dress up with our school uniforms. We felt quite posh. For our teatime, we had baked beans on toast, and Battenberg cake for a treat, something Karen and I had never had before, it was yummy. After tea, my sister and I played outside while our mother set about laying down the new carpet, and making up our bed with the new blankets. That night we went to bed with full bellies and slept in a warm bed.

The next day, we were up early as my mother was ready to whitewash the inside of the bus. Removing all the old curtains, she then gave the walls and ceiling another good wash. Two hours later, she was finished with the painting, and hung up her brightly coloured poke-a-dot curtains. Steve and Jill did not care to use the outhouse, they preferred the great outdoors, said it smelt a whole lot fresher. My mother however, was inclined to a little more privacy and with the left over paint she gave the inside of the outhouse a once over. My sister and I did not like to use the "black-hole," either and only went to the outhouse for a number two when accompanied by our mum. For emergencies at night, my mother kept a potty under the bed. After taking a short lunch break, she then took a bucket of hot soapy water and attacked the outside of the bus, washing off as much of the green slime and soot as she could that had accumulated over the years.

There wasn't a day went by that there was not a pot of water boiling on the stove, ready for bathing, washing clothes or for doing the dishes. With the cold rainy days of winter setting in, it was necessary sometimes for my mother to hang her washing inside the bus. At times, it resembled a Chinese laundry. With steamed up windows, the smoky smell of the wood burning, a waxy odour of candles, and the faint whiff of mildew, it was not always a pleasant place to be at times, but it was home. It was not long until the mice problems subsided, although the odd one did still meet its demise under our bed.

It was on one such morning, that Mrs. Housdan paid us the first of many visits. I did not realize it at the time, but looking back on that old bus, I can only imagine my mum's discomfort at that situation. She tried to explain to Mrs. Housdan, the circumstances of her living conditions, who took it all in stride. Taking up my mother's offer, she sat down for a cup of tea. Mrs. Housdan had come to let my mother know that school had been arranged for the following Monday. She told my mother that she would be at the bus first thing Monday morning to pick us up for school, and introduce us to the head mistress. She then inquired as to whether my mother had managed to pick up our school uniforms, which my sister and I were only to pleased to model for her

That weekend rolled by all too fast and fear of the unknown started to turn my stomach in knots. A fact that did not go unnoticed by my mother as she tried to deal with our concerns about this new phase of our life. She assured us she would also come to school with us that morning, and would be there to pick us up in the afternoon.

School did not go well for me at first. The days were long and as I was only four at the time, I found the work hard to comprehend. Older boys were unkind and bullied me when my sister was not around, so I tended to stay close to her and her friends, which did not help with the teasing. I think the fact that we lived in a bus put us off from making any close friends. The thought of someone wanting to come over and play was enough to curb any close friendships.

Mrs. Housdan continued to visit my mum on a regular basis, always bringing Karen and I a little treat each time. There were times when we would all visit together and other times when Mrs. Housdan would ask Karen and me to go outside and play while they talked. These private meetings would always leave my mother down in the dumps. It was not until years later did we learned the significance of some of those meetings. Mrs. Housdan, in her wisdom, had set in motion a foster home for Karen and me to go live in. This would have been a temporary situation until my mother could find work and get back on her feet. All Mrs. Housdan needed was my mother's consent to have us removed from the bus. The very idea my mother could not fathom and absolutely rejected. At one point, there was a veiled threat by Mrs. Housdan. All she needed was a court order and she could have us removed from the bus if necessary. This put a real strain on what had been a close friendship between the two of them. The last ten years had seen my mother deal with the passing of her own mum, the stress of five long years of war while living in London and the break-up of her own marriage. The removal of Karen and John from the home now would be the most unbearable of all situations for her as she struggled to get her life back on track. Pleading with Mrs. Housdan, she told her "Those kids are my life, my only reason for living; you take them away from me now and I will have no reason to carry on, nothing left to work for." Overwhelmed by the thought of losing Karen and me for any length of time, my mother came down with a threat of her own, and it was not a veiled one at that. She warned Mrs. Housdan, that if anyone ever came for Karen and John, they would have to go through her and it would not be pretty. She then asked Mrs. Housdan to leave.

We spent most of our free time at gypsy Steve's camp. They always had a campfire on the go, which was a big draw for my sister and me. We liked to watch them cook their meals in a big black pot over the open fire. Steve was a superb forager; scouring the hedgerows in search of nuts and roots of plants that would enhance his food. Some meals could be a real hotchpotch. Left over rabbit stew from one day might have a few more vegetables added the next day or maybe a squirrel or two the following day. He also had his own traditional remedies for sickness: rose hip tea for colds and sore throats, hops for their infection fighting ingredients, digestion, and relaxing effects. Sleeping on a pillow full of hops he said was a good cure for insomnia. Tea made from stinging nettles would settle an upset stomach. The dandelion wine Steve made though, he used mostly for his own medicinal purpose. Our favourite was the chestnut, roasted on an open fire at night was always a treat for us. We also watch Jill as she made wooden clothes pegs. Carved out of a six-inch long stick of wood, split up the middle and with a sliver of tin wrapped around one end. My mother always said that that style of peg was the best she ever used. Jill also liked to weave neat little baskets out of willow branches. From time to time, she would take these items into town and sell them for cash or bartered for goods.

In the spring, Jill would pick wild flowers, snowdrops, primroses, and violets to sell in town for extra cash. There was an abundance of wildlife in the woods around Monkery Bottom too, and Steve had no problem hunting them. Rabbit, squirrel, hedgehog and pheasant were just a few of the things he would show up with some days.

The hedgehog was prepared in rather a bizarre fashion. When cornered, these little critters would roll up into a small ball for protection, leaving their spiny coat exposed. Steve would then pack the spiny outer shell in clay and throw it into the fire to bake. When the clay had hardened, he would then take them out of the fire and break away the clay, thus removing the hedgehog's prickly outer shell and leaving the cooked meat inside.

One evening, while sitting around the fire, my mother asked Steve how he managed to catch pheasants. Knowing he was a good shot with a catapult, she thought that might be his answer. However, he explained to my mother that he would pick a few choice places in the fields and lay down grain in the evening. It would be the same spot each day for a week.

On the final day, he would soak the grain in some home brew. The birds, having developed the habit of returning to the same place each day, would eat the grain, become intoxicated and unable to fly. According to Steve, you could just go and pick them up. I don't know if my mother ever believed that story. She tended to think he poached them from one of the local farms in the vicinity that bred pheasants.

Steve was not above sharing the odd rabbit or chicken with my mother, which helped contribute to the food budget. From time to time, my mother would repay the favour with one of her famed old fashion English Bread Puddings. Steve also directed my mother to a potato field a half mile down the road. Climbing through the hedge, she would pull just enough potatoes for a couple of meal. Bubble and squeak, potato pancakes or a bowl of tomato soup with a large scoop of mash potato in the middle became some of my mother's old standbys for a cheap meal.

It was not long though before the farmer harvested the field. Potato picking now became a family affair as my mother, sister and I scoured the field looking for any potatoes missed by the pickers. These would be ones that were either too small for market or had been sliced in two by the digger.

Friday night, cold, wet and hungry, we had returned from the potato patch, filled our tummies with tomato soup and mash, and retired to bed early. With the rain gently tapping on the metal roof of the bus and a soft warm glow coming from the wood stove, it was not long before we drifted off to sleep. Sometime later, a loud knock at the door startled us. Rising cautiously from the bed my mother called out, "Whose there?" "It's Ed and Billy, Jim's boys! Dad sent us down to collect the rent." As it was Friday night, the thought crossed my mother's mind that the boys might be looking for beer money. Lighting a candle she held it up to the rain-spattered glass of the buses front door. In the shadows, she could make out the faces of two men standing just outside the entrance, both soaked to the skin. Again, she asked them to state their business. "Dad sent us down to collect the rent. Okay!" grunted the older one again. "Rent's not due till tomorrow," my mother replied, "so you best clear off and come back in the morning." Then suddenly, with a cuss and a swift kick, the door flew open. Standing at the entrance of the bus was the elder of the two boys. He had small close-set eyes and a vacant look; one of his arms was missing at the elbow. His brother, a skinny runt, cowardly hovered behind him. Brazenly, the elder one stuck his head inside the bus door; looking around he again demanded the five shillings rent. My mother, now on her guard told him again, "The rents not due till tomorrow," and upping her tone, told them to "piss off," giving the door a push to shut it. Again, he kicked the door back open and putting one foot inside as he spoke, "If ya can't pay the bloody rent Misses I'll just have to take that carpet!" My mother, squaring her shoulders, grabbed a knife off the counter and waving it in his face, blurted out. "Take one more step inside mate and you'll lose the other god-dam arm, now piss off!" Staggered by the show of aggression, he stepped back off the bus, cussing at my mother in the process, and vowing to come back again.

For fear they might return, my mother slid the door closed and jammed a chair into the stairwell of the bus. Blowing out the candle, she sat down by the door for a good while, making sure they had left. Coming back to bed, she laid the knife down on the floor beside her. Calming our fears, she climbed back into bed. However, she did not sleep easy for the rest of the night.

Christmas was now less than a week away. Karen and I had been busy at school making paper chains and bringing them home to decorate the bus. My mother had started baking some of her cakes and biscuits and things began to look and feel quite festive. At my age, I do not remember having any concept of the giving or receiving of gifts for Christmas, but I do have one very vivid memory of that first Christmas we spent in the bus at Monkery Bottom.

It was one of those dismal December nights. We had been in Ashford most of the day while my mother did the last of her Christmas shopping. We had missed the Canterbury bus, which meant we would have a long walk up Charing Hill. It was dark, and we were cold, wet and hungry by the time we reached home. Once inside the bus, my mother soon got a fire going and put the kettle on. After a quick cup of tea and a bowl of soup we were off to bed. My mother had no sooner blown out the candles than the lights of a car lit up the inside of the bus. Slipping out of bed, she quickly checked to make sure the chair was secure in the stairwell. Then grabbing a knife from the draw she crept back to the bed, sat down and waited. There was the muffled sound of voices outside, then a knock at the door. Looking outside, my mother could see the silhouette of two figures, standing by the bus door, back lit by the headlights of the car. Fearing the worst, she yelled out, "Piss off, ya hear!" There were a few more muffled tones then a friendly voice call out to her by name, "Mrs Roders." "State your business," she said in an angry manner. "It's Captain Dan of the Salvation Army and Rose my wife. We've come to bring you some Christmas cheer," shinning his torch on two large parcels they were holding. Wiping the mist from the window, my mother could just make out the uniform of the Army. Removing the chair from the stairwell, she opened the door and motioned for them to come in. Quickly finding a match, she lit some candles and placed another log on the fire.

As they seated themselves at the table, my mother began to explain the circumstances that had led to her rude behaviour. While they sat drinking tea, she recounted the events of that evening when the two drunks had shown up at our door looking for beer money. Captain Dan mentioned that he knew the father of the two boys and that he would have a word with him and assured my mother that the situation would not occur again. After tea, and some chitchat, Captain Dan told my mother that he would keep an eye open as to any job situations that might be of interest to her. Then after a short prayer time, he wished us a Merry Christmas and hoped that we would enjoy our boxes of Christmas cheer.

The very boxes my sister and I had been eyeing for the last half-hour. I do not think we had ever seen parcels wrapped so beautifully and in so many bright colors. With all the excitement, it was hard to get back to sleep. Christmas had now taken on a completely new meaning, and we could not wait for the next few days to go by.

In the morning, my mother put the box with the presents under the bed. The one filled with fruit, nuts, cake, and sweets, we helped her unpack and put away. So much food we had never seen the likes of before.

When Christmas comes around each year, I always reflect back on the one we spent at Monkery Bottom. It was my first memory of Christmas as a child, and when I reflect back on it, I remember the kindness of others: the generosity of Steve and Jill, how they had helped supplemented my mother's food budget; Taffy, for his never-ending supply of firewood that kept us warm for that winter, with very little payment.

Mrs. Housdan, who helped my mother out when she was at her lowest possible ebb, the Salvation Army for their comfort to us that first Christmas, and my mother, who under the most trying conditions, made a home for us in that old bus and put together the first Christmas Karen and I remember.

Chapter 7

Charing

...a flower in the garden of England.

In the midst of those cold and gloomy winter nights, with no radio or television for entertainment, it was usually early to bed for us. Lying there, Karen and I would often fall asleep to the sound of our mother's voice as she read to us by candle light. Stories out of old Readers Digest magazines were always a favourite. "So Long Voyager," was a story about an injured Canada goose that a couple had nursed back to health over the winter months. Then, in the spring, they bid the goose a tearful good-bye as it flew north to join its flock. This was just one of the many stories I remember.

There were nights, while lying in bed listening to the winter storm howl around outside, a gust of wind would sometimes whistle down the chimney and fill the inside of the bus with smoke. The sound of cardboard popping out of a window would send my mother scrambling from the bed to patch up the hole; stopping the icy winds from blowing in. When the moon was full, it would light up the inside of the bus, others nights, it was so dark you could not see a hand in front of your face. In those dark, quiet nights, the only sounds you could hear were the hiss and crackle of a log in the woodstove, or the rare haunting hoot of a night owl on the hunt. This sound would send Karen and me diving under the covers. Occasionally, the trumpeting sounds of the horses, as they released their intestinal gases would send us off in fits of laughter.

Many times we would ask our mother to tell us stories about her growing up in London. The time she had watched her father march of to war, returning home two years later, shell-shocked, toes missing from frostbite and jobless. The only solace he found was in a bottle. With a physically and verbally abusive father and eight mouths to feed, how her mother had struggled to keep house, home and a marriage together. As kids, how they had run through the fish-market and stealthy stuck out a hand to grab a fish or two. Times they had lined up at the slaughterhouse looking for a bag of cows ears. In away, these stories were a comfort to my sister and me. We had a loving mother, a roof over our heads, clothing and food on the table.

On the lighter side, she would sometimes entertain us by speculating on the history of the old bus: stories of places it might have been, or the people who may have traveled on it, paupers, peasants, the rich and wealthy, even royalty, maybe! As kids, lying there in the open shell of the old bus, our imaginations running wild, we liked to think it all could have happened. How or why it had ended up in the middle of nowhere, in a dirt lay-by at Monkery Bottom, she could never really figured out., Although, each time she would paint a different picture about the bus's circumstance.

Sometimes, Karen and I would question our mother as to the whereabouts of our father, why we never saw him, or why he never came to visit us. Her standard answer was always the same: they had fallen out of love and he had decided to stay in Holland, that Holland was a long way away. He would come visit us when he was ready, but he never did. *It would be many years before my sister and I would finally meet our father.*

In our early years, my mother never talked about any of his abusive ways, or how he had tried to separate Karen and me at an early age. Therefore, we never grew up with any opinion as to what kind of man our father really was. The only times we ever heard our mother mean-mouth our dad, was when she went to pick up her alimony and it would not be there or it was late.

As the old year slipped away, and the days grew longer, my

mother watched the approach of spring with a new optimism. Lying in bed in the early hours of a spring morning, the sun lighting up the inside of the bus, she thought about what Mrs. Housdan had told her a few months ago. The Ashford Council were serious about building a new housing estate in Hothfield, just a few miles down the road from Charing. As soon as the finances were in place, the housing project would go ahead. Part of the governments plan was to get some of the gypsy population off the roads and families displaced by the war into permanent housing. Mrs. Housdan told my mother there was a good chance she would qualify for one of these new council houses.

With that thought in mind, my mother was determined not to spend another minute at Monkery Bottom and resolved to find work as soon as possible. Steve and Jill were already out of bed, ready to start their morning chores. The crackle of their fire was a good indication the kettle was already on for a pot of tea. Following breakfast and a cup of tea with Steve and Jill, my mother turned her enthusiasm into spring-cleaning. Taking all the old cardboard out of the windows to let in some fresh air, she began to give the inside of the bus a good clean. Karen and I removed all the old furnishings while my mother went to work on the floor with the scrub brush. She finished up just as Jill returned from an early morning walk in the woods; she had been out gathering wild flowers. Putting the kettle on for another pot of tea, she called my mum over to take a break. As they sat drinking tea and chitchatting, Jill made up her bouquets of wild flowers, ready to take to town later that morning. "I heard a Cuckoo this morning Tilly, that's a sure sign of spring you know." My mother nodded knowingly, as the only sounds she had heard that morning was the sound of a scrub brush on metal as she scoured the bus floor.

Steve had been out early too, checking his snares. He arrived back home with a rabbit. After gutting and skinning it, he offered to make dinner that afternoon, for which my mother was grateful. While they sat there talking and puffing on a fag, Steve mentioned that it would soon be time for them to be moving on: time to pull up stakes and look for some itinerant farm work. This made my mother rather sad, as they had been such a help and comfort to her over the winter.

Finishing her cup of tea and cigarette, my mother was ready to get back to her cleaning just as Mrs. Housdan drove into the enclosure. She had not been around now for a couple of weeks, and the last time my mother dropped in to see her, she had been out of town. As she exited the car, Karen and I ran up to greet her in anticipation of some sweets. She did not disappoint us. With the usual good-natured hellos out of the way, Mrs. Housdan asked my mother if she could have a word with her in private. She told Karen and me to stay seated by the fire. Getting up, my mother gave Steve and Jill a moues look, rolled her eyes, and followed on behind her. Thoughts of the court order for the removal of Karen and John from the home flashed through my mother's mind. Fear of that likelihood had troubled her all winter. Feeling anxious and a little weak at the knees, she followed Mrs. Housdan over to the bus. Was it time to pack up the kids and leave? Where would they go? Should she go back to London, back to the restaurant where she had worked before the war? Where would they stay? Maybe Old Aunt Rose would put them up. Walking toward the bus, a range of thoughts and emotions raced through my mother's head. Her mind in a turmoil.

"Tilly, shall we have a seat?" Mrs. Housdan asked, looking at my mother rather strangely. It was at that moment, my mother realized they had come to a stop, and she was standing there lost in thought. "Oh yes, by all means. I'll put the kettle on for tea." "No thank Tilly," said Mrs. Housdan. "When I tell you what I have to say, we won't have time for tea." The words rang in my mother's ears. Her legs felt like rubber, too weak to stand, as she sank into the chair beside Mrs. Housdan. "Well, what is it?" my mother asked abruptly, not for one minute wanting to hear what she had to say. "I've found you a job, Tilly," she said. My mother sat there dumbstruck, wondering if she had heard her right. "You will be working *In Service* down in the village of Charing for a family of four, a Colonel Dagueneau, his wife and their two daughters. The girls are about the same age as Karen and John. It's a cook's position, with some light housekeeping duties. Do you think that would be suitable for you, Tilly?" My mother sat there speechless, not quite sure what to think or say. "Well Tilly!" Mrs. Housdan prompted. "Well, I don't know. It sounds almost too good to be true, but yes, Oh, yes! That sounds wonderful. When do I start?" "Well, you'll need to get changed first and then I'll take you down for the interview."

While Karen and I sat around the fire with our sweets, talking with Jill and Steve, we could see my mother sitting outside the bus talking with Mrs. Housdan. Steve and Jill had delayed their trip to the town; they were waiting to see what the outcome of the meeting would be. Unbeknownst to Karen and me, my mother had made them aware of the situation with the foster home, and they were ready to help my mother out in any way they could, if the need should arise. Suddenly, there was a shriek of excitement from my mother. It was hard to tell if it was one of delight or disaster. Then jumping up, she ran to where we sat. "Karen, John, get over here right now!" She hollered. Calling over our heads to Steve and Jill, "I have a job; I'll tell you all about it when I get back." With a quick spit and polish, my mother had us into our school uniforms, the only decent clothes we had at the time. Then we were off to Charing for my mother's interview.

The Dagueneaus were a well-to-do family, who lived at the bottom of Charing Hill. Turning left off Canterbury Road and heading into the village, Mrs. Housdan made a sharp right turn up a long gravel driveway lined with rhododendron bushes down one side. The large private grounds had well-manicured lawns, with numerous attractive flowerbeds. Mrs. Housdan asked us to wait in the car while she went and knocked on the side door. Mr. Dagueneau answered it. He was a tall, well-built man, in his mid fifties, with thin brownish grey hair and an austere manner. Invited into the house, he showed us into the living room where he introduced his wife, Mrs. Dagueneau. She was a slim, regal-looking woman, prim and proper, and a little on the reticent side.

While my mother went through her interview process, Mrs. Housdan took Karen and me back outside and showed us around the gardens. The Dagueneau girls, for some reason, had decided to make themselves scarce, except for the occasional glance out of an upstairs' window. During the interview process, my mother was questioned about her cooking experience, her familiarity with certain foods and her ability to prepare them. On a tour of the house, starting with the kitchen, Mrs. Dagueneau showed my mother the menu she had made up for the week. She would need to shop each day, and prepare those meals. Sunday dinner would be the traditional roast beef and Yorkshire pudding with all the trimmings. For dessert, pie was a favourite with the family, and depending on the season, it could be apple, cherry or blackberry with homemade custard.

After the hour-long interview the Dagueneaus' agreed that my mother could have the job and she could start the following Monday. This would give us a few days to pack. Mr. Dagueneau planned to be at Monkery Bottom around eight o'clock Sunday morning to help with the move. The thought of him seeing our old bus did not appeal to my mother and she suggested that she could make her own way to Charing on Sunday. Mr. Dagueneau dismissed the suggestion, as he needed my mother to be there in time to take stock of the pantry and prepare meals for Monday.

On the way back to "Monkery Bottom," my mother thanked Mrs. Housdan for all she had done. She told my mother she would continue to keep in touch with her and if she had any concerns about her work situation, to let her know. She also told my mother she would be at the Dagueneaus' 8:30, Monday morning to arrange for the change of schooling for Karen and me to Charing Primary School.

Back at Monkery Bottom, things were deserted. Steve and Jill had now gone to town to sell her bouquets of wild flowers. Our furnishings still sat outside the bus, left there in our haste to get ready for my mother's job interview. Sitting by a dying fire, my mother, excited at the prospect of her new job, suddenly, jumped up. "Come on kids!" she said, "let's put this stuff back in the bus and we'll go to Ashford and celebrate." Ten minutes later, we were off down the road again, heading for Charing to catch a bus into Ashford. Back in the village, we took a long slow walk past the Dagueneau's house, the place we would soon call home.

Sunday morning was a melancholy time for us as we sat around the campfire for the last time with our cups of tea. My mother explained to Steve and Jill what her duties would be while working in service for the Colonel. "You're not goin ta go all la-de-da on us now are ya Tilly," quipped Jill. Taffy, the old boy from down the road, who had kept us in firewood for the past six months with very little payment dropped by to wish us well. He gave my sister and me another one of his home made *"Monkey on a Stick,"* a toy he was well known for making. The few belongings my mother had that she no longer needed, she distributed between them. She thanked Steve and Jill for their kindness and generosity to us over the winter and gave them some extra food she no longer needed. A couple of old pots and some dishes plus the carpet she gave to Taffy. The notorious piece of carpeting that could have been grounds for some blood shed, even murder. "Better you get the carpet Taffy than those other two drunken bastards," my mother said, and they all had a good laugh.

Mr. Dagueneau showed up at eight o'clock that morning driving a sporty Jaguar convertible. He made very little conversation as he piled our few belongings into the boot of his car. With final hugs goodbye, we were on our way.

My mother always said she left Monkery Bottom a brighter place than when she found it. The bus was no longer the unsightly, rusting hulk, it had once been. It now stood boldly in its place, as if it were entitled to be there. The chestnut tree growing out of the engine compartment was now in full leaf and added a rather exotic flavour to the place. The whitewashed exterior, with the large red poker-dot curtains, and school artwork left littering the windows made for a colourful sight. Not the caravan my mother had expected to rent at Monkery Bottom. Just an old bus, getting on in years, looking for someone to make a home in it, and make it a home she did. Yes! Without a doubt, she did leave Monkery Bottom a brighter place than she did find it.

Taking a last look back, I saw Steve and Jill's brightly painted wagon covered in early morning dew. The horses stood statuesque in the sweet light of a misty spring morning; their white breath mingled, and hung in the air. The big, black pot suspended by the fire, ready for some tasty delight, a pleasure we had shared in so many times. With these sights, sounds and smells in my mind, I saw a curtain fluttering out of an open window of the bus. It seemed to be giving us a final wave goodbye. Pulling out of the dirt lay-by, the Colonel's Jag purred up the road toward Charing. It was an odd contrast to how we had arrived just six months earlier.

It had been a long, cold winter at Monkery Bottom and my mother was ready for a fresh start. This was an opportunity for her to put her life and profession as a cook back on track. With a high social status and well respected in the community, my mother felt fortunate to be in the Colonel's employment and entrusted with their domestic and culinary affairs.

The village of Charing lay below us in the valley, located on the south slope of the North Downs, along Pilgrims Way. Much of the village has not changed in six hundred years. Shops and homes, with oriel windows still overlooked the narrow main street. Many of the buildings built back in the sixteenth century are still in commercial use today. The church of Saint Peter and Saint Paul in the village dates back to the early thirteenth century and almost destroyed by a fire in 1590. Some hotshot from the gun of a hunter hit the roof, setting the shingles of the church on fire and leaving only the walls standing. The church was eventually rebuilt.

Arriving at the house, Mr. Dagueneau showed us to our living quarters on the second floor. It was a large bed-sitting room, with double bed, a big easy chair sat in one corner. Beside the chair was a small table with a radio on it. A large wardrobe stood on the opposite side of the room. Against the wall at the foot of the bed was an old oak dressing table with a marble top. Mr. Dagueneau asked that we turn off all lights and the radio if there was nobody in the room. Down the hall, he showed us the toilet, and bathroom with hot and cold running water. After the brief tour, Mr. Dagueneau asked us to join him downstairs in the sitting room as soon as we had unpacked. It was hard for my sister and me to contain our excitement of living in such a beautiful house. My mother quickly unpacked, fixed herself up and prepared to go downstairs. In the sitting room, Mr. Dagueneau officially introduced us to his two daughters, Veronica and Jennifer. He then suggested that Karen and I should run along and play with the girls while he and his wife met with my mother.

One of the rooms in the house was a dedicated playroom. Here, there were many toys and games to play with, although not much in the way of toys for a boy. The girls were very out going and friendly in a posh kind of way. When they showed us around the garden, I saw a swing set and a tricycle in the backyard that was more to my liking. Their father did not allow any children from the village to come play in the garden, and the girls were not permit to play outside the garden. This was a rule their father strictly enforced. Karen and I would now become their built-in playmates.

On a tour of the house, Mrs. Dagueneau let my mother know that everyday there should be fresh cut flowers in the dining room and a decanter of water on the bar in the sitting room in the evening. The house would be off limits to us with the exception of the kitchen area, where we would eat our meals, the playroom and the garden. Mrs. Dagueneau explained to my mother that her day would start at six in the morning, to be ready for a seven o'clock breakfast. Eggs soft boiled, lightly buttered toast and marmalade would be the standard fare, with cereal for the girls. Dinner, served at twelve noon, with a set menu given to my mother at the beginning of each week. Tea would be served at four thirty, with an assortment of sandwiches, soup and a light dessert. Following cleanup of the tea dishes, my mother would be finished for the day. There would be a light snack in the evening that the Dagueneaus' would look after for themselves. If my mother had no more questions, she could have the rest of the day to take stock of the pantry and familiarize herself with the kitchen. That evening we took our first bathe in a real bathtub. With hot running water, electric lights, heater, and a radio to listen to when we went to bed. *The Archers, Journey into Space and the Goon Show,* were just a few of the programs we enjoyed.

Monday morning, Mrs. Housdan arrived at the Dagueneaus' residence to take us down the school to register. Run by the Church of England, Charing Primary had an emphasis on Christian education. On the weekend, students were encouraged to attend Sunday school at the local church. During the registration, the Head Master pointed out to my mum that school uniforms were required. Mrs. Housdan told my mother that it would not be a problem. She could take us into Ashford that afternoon and pick them up.

Tuesday morning, we were up early for our first day at Charing School. It was a short walk from Dagueneaus house, through the village to the school, with a quick stop at the park to play on the swings if we were early. On Sundays, our mother would take us down to the church for our Sunday school lessons. It consisted mostly of bible stories, arts and craft, and memorization of the catechism. Our attendance at Sunday school was noted with a large colourful stamp pasted in our lesson book.

The Dagueneau house was an impressive place to call home and for the first time we had no embarrassment as to where we lived. The job was going well for my mother, and shopping in the village, she had made friends with a number of the shopkeepers and their staff. Dagueneaus' were satisfied with her cooking and cleaning and Karen and I got along well with the girls. Many times the girls preferred to eat in the kitchen with us, and for a time their parents went along with this arrangement.

With life now settling down to some resemblance of normality, my mother decided that she would celebrate Karen's and my birthdays. For Karen, who was turning six and I was turning five this would be our first birthday celebration. With steady work now and a little extra money, my mother bought me a pedal car; the very one I had been pining over ever since I first set eyes on it in Ashford last Christmas. My sister wanted a bike, but settled for a scooter.

At school, we began to make new friends, who found it unusual that they could not come to the house and play. Because of this, we did not always come home right after school. Sometimes we would stop at the park or play around in the village. This started to cause a little friction between the Dagueneau girls and us as they expected Karen and me to come home right after school and be with them.

It was on one such occasion, while we were playing in

the village, Mr. Dagueneau happened to drive past. Noticing Karen and me playing with our friends, he called us over and told us it was not a good idea to be running around the streets. He suggested we get along home right away. My mother, hearing of this situation, informed Mr. Dagueneau that she did not have a problem with Karen and me playing with our friends in the village. In future, she told him, if there were any difficulties concerning Karen and John, he was to let her know and she would deal with it. This disagreement over authority of my sister and me in the house did not sit well with Mr. Dagueneau. It affected our relationship with him and the girls for a time, as they felt we were rejecting their friendship.

To keep the peace, my mother suggested that we come home from school first and then go out to play after tea. This worked well for a while until one day after school, as we were standing outside the main gate of the house talking with some of our friends, Mr. Dagueneau happened to come home early. He told Karen, his daughters and me to go inside the house. He then advise the rest of the kids he did not want them loitering outside the gate, so they best be on there way. Back in the house, Mr. Dagueneau lectured us again about staying away from the front gate so as not to entice kids to hang around out there. Again, my mother was not pleased with the situation, but she did convey to Karen and me Mr Dagueneau's concern. She asked that we follow his rules to help keep the peace.

With the summer coming on and the weather turning warmer, my mother looked around for things to do on the weekends that would give us all a break from the house. Hiking the North Downs, with a picnic basket was always a favourite pastime. From the top of Charing Hill, it was possible to see for miles across the rolling countryside and farmlands of Kent. Sitting there in the tranquillity of the moment, the sounds of the village church bells would occasionally break the silence.

It was here one day, we learned from an old timer about the underground army in Charing, how it operated as part of the Home Guard during the war. It was so secret that there were no official papers existing for this 203rd Kent Battalion, their activities known only to each other. Even their families had no knowledge of their activities. These patrols consisted of a leader and six or seven men, operating out of secret underground hideouts and observation posts. One of these hideouts was located at the top of Charing Hill under an old drinking trough. Another larger one was located at Chollock. The plan was to sabotage any German supply routes if they made it into England. They also removed all road signs so as not to give the German army any directions to London.

On the way home, we would walk back through the woods along Pilgrims Way, with its array of refreshing scented vines, multi-coloured wild flowers and wild herbs. Out on the grassy slopes, my sister and I liked to play a game we called *"Rolley-Polley."* A game we had played many times before to see who could roll down the tall grassy slopes the fastest. This time though, while rolling through the towering grass ahead of Karen, I had by chance disturbed a snake. Unaware of the situation, and following close behind me, Karen rolled right into the path of the adder. Striking her in the upper thigh, she grabbed her leg in pain, briefly trapping the snake in her dress. "Help me mummy!" she shriek. Confused for a moment by all the excitement, I was panic-stricken myself when I saw the snake fall to the ground. Our mother, running down the hill arrived just as the snake, now in full retreat slithered off through the grass. Grabbing Karen's leg, she began to suck on the snakebite in hopes of drawing out as much of the poison as possible. With my sister, now in shock, and shaking hysterically, we ran from the field into Charing to seek medical help.

At the surgery, Dr. Littledale gave her an antidote for the bite, and a sedative to calm her down. The next morning, still in shock and unable to walk, she had to use a wheelchair to get around. After a few days of healing at home, she went back to school and found herself an instant celebrity. None of the teachers or students had ever known of anyone bitten by a snake before. At recess, there was no shortage of friends willing to push this celebrated student around the playground in her wheelchair.

After the snakebite, we had no more desire to go back to the Downs. Instead, my mother decided that the seaside might be a better choice. To cheer Karen up, she began to make plans for an outing on Whitsunday, just a couple of weeks away.

With my sister fully recovered from her physical experience with the snake, the time had come for our seaside outing. Rising early that morning, my mother packed a picnic basket and we were on our way. This would be the first time we had ever been to the beach and before setting off my mother gave Karen and me a half-crown each for pocket money. Sitting upstairs on the bus, we amused ourselves by deciding what to do with the money when we got to the seaside. I had decided on a bucket and spade and my sister wanted a beach ball.

There was a great deal of excitement with the other kids on the bus when we caught our first glimpse of a sun-speckled sea in the distance. Getting off the bus, we shuffled along with the crowd as we made our way toward the beach. The sound of slapping waves, squawking seagulls and the hurdy-gurdy man echoed in the air. Along the promenade, shops were brightly decorated with there flags and streamers. Young people made their way along the boulevards, laughing as they stopped to read the smutty postcards on stands outside the shops. Others were sticking coins into slot machine to see *"What the Butler Saw."* Young children sucking on giant peppermint rocks and ice cream cones dragged their heels as they tried to take in all the excitement. With a quick stop at one of the many souvenir stores, I picked up my bucket and spade, Karen her beach ball and for my mother, a sun hat. Down at the beachfront my mother rented herself a deckchair and found a shady spot up against the sea wall. She was quite happy to sit there, read her newspaper and do the crossword puzzle. After a few hours of building sand castles, paddling in the tidal pools and chasing crabs, we took a ride on the donkeys. Looking into the soft gentle eyes of one of them, I couldn't help thinking back to *Hillside Farm* and wondering how, Funny Face was doing and if she ever missed us.

Lunchtime, my mother unpacked our picnic basket, filled with corned beef sandwiches, hard-boiled eggs and a large bottle of Tizer. While we sat there eating our lunch, a clown came by promoting a *"Punch and Judy Show,"* that would be starting in a half-hour.

After lunch and with an ice cream in hand, we wandered down the beach to watch the hilarious antics of Punch as he scolded his poor wife Judy, over many a petty and trivial matter. Kids sat on the sand, either taking Punch or Judy's side of the arguments, with much booing or hissing, and in return lots of backchat from Punch and Judy. Following the show, we walked the promenade in search of a fish-n-chip shop for our supper. Then with the essential stick of rock with the name through the center, we were on our way home.

Returning home to Charing, after a fun-filled day at the seaside, we made our mother promise to take us back again soon. Tired and pooped out from a long day, we went right up to our room and my mother gave us a bath before settling us down for the night. A few minutes later, Mr. Dagueneau came up the stairs and without so much as a how do you do, asked my mother to come downstairs as soon as she had us settled, as he wished to speak with her. Rolling her eyes, she finished our bath, tucked us into bed and went downstairs to the sitting room where the Dagueneaus' were waiting.

It appeared that, while we were away for the day, some local kids he believed to be friends of Karen and mine had come into the garden, and according to Mr. Dagueneau, had harassed his daughters. When he asked them to leave, they did not go quietly and were ill mannered and rude to him as well. A pointed finger silenced my mother as she tried to question him. "One minute," Mr. Dagueneau said, his voice now becoming more elevated and superior in tone that my sister and I could hear him all the way upstairs. "I do not want Karen or John playing in the village any more. They are attracting too many ruffians to the house, so I would appreciate it if they came home right after school from now on and stayed home." My mother, annoyed with his high and mighty attitude, was ready to have her say. Again, clearing his throat, Mr. Dagueneau excused himself once more to make a final point. "Furthermore," he said, "I do not want my girls eating in the kitchen anymore as they seem to be picking up too many bad habits." By now, my mother had had enough of Mr. Dagueneau and his pompous attitude. With her Cockney Irish dander up, she was ready to have her say. "As for the kids in the garden, I have no idea who they might be, or do I care. I have no control over things that happen around this house on my days off. What's more, I know who Karen and John's friends are in the village and I know the parents, their kids are not ruffians. Karen and John are going to have to make their own way in life sometime, and they need to associate with other people outside these four walls. As far as their school friends go, they are more kith and kin than your two girls, and I have no problem with Karen and John playing with them in the village." She then told Mr. Dagueneau, "I do not put up with any bad behaviour in the kitchen, from your girls or Karen and John. As for manners, maybe the girls do not always hold their knife and fork correctly, or dip their soupspoon in the right side of the bowl. This is not bad manners, maybe just not good etiquette. As far as discipline goes, maybe you should get busy with the girls, as I do not see that as part of my job." With that, she bade them a hasty "Goodnight," and took her leave.

Coming back upstairs, the thought went through my mother's mind that she may have gone a little too far. Her feelings confirmed a few minutes later when Mr. Dagueneau came back upstairs and told my mother that he was discharging her from his employment with them, and she was to be out of the house by Monday.

How could such a fun and exciting day have spiralled so quickly out of control? My mother assured us that everything would be all right and not to worry. In the morning, after a long restless night she apologetically pleaded with Mr. Dagueneau to get her job back, but to no avail. His only response was to confirm the fact that she was to be out of the house in the morning.

Monday morning, my mother packed our bags and we walked out of the Dagueneaus' house for the last time and into Charing to catch the bus to Ashford. There my mother expected to see Mrs. Housdan and speak to her about finding us a place to live. Arriving in Ashford, a little before noon, we headed for her office. There, they told my mother that Mrs. Housdan was out of the office and not expected back until the morning. Explaining her situation to the clerk, my mother told her that we would need a place to live in before the end of the day. She in turn, explained to my mother that there were not a lot of living spaces available for single parents. Much of their accommodation was for two parent families with two or more children. If she could come back after lunch, they would see what they could do for her.

Following lunch, we returned to the office in hopes that somebody might have found us a suitable place to rent. Instead, they gave my mother a number of forms to fill out for their records. After interviewing her and checking her case file, they suggested that she should go register in with the Salvation Army Shelter, just in case they were unable to find us any suitable accommodation. On that point, my mother made it quite clear to them that she would not be going anywhere until they found us a place to live.

By three thirty and with no signs of housing, one of the staff reminded my mother that the office would be closing at four thirty. One of the office employees had taken it upon themselves to inform the shelter that we were in their office and that they should make provisions for the three of us for the night. At four-thirty, the clerk made it known to my mother that the office was now closing, and that there was a reservation for us at the shelter and we were to make our way over there. She could then return in the morning to speak to Mrs. Housdan. My mother, refusing to leave the office, told them she was prepared to spend the night in the office if they did not find us a place. They in turn advised my mother that if she did not leave the office immediately, they would apprehend the children and arrested her for trespassing. Again, they asked my mother to leave the office, go to the Salvation Army Shelter, and return in the morning.

Steadfast in her resolve, she defied anyone to touch either her, or her children. "Find us a place, or we are here for the night," was her final words. So there we sat, listening to muffled voices behind closed doors making last minute phone calls. At five thirty, tired and hungry after a long afternoon in the office, a supervisor came out to the waiting room and asked us to go with him. Questioning the official as to where he was taking us, he told my mother they had found us a place at Hothfield Hut Camp and that someone would drive us there.

Chapter 8

Hothfield Hut Camp

There were know pretences among us,
we were all in the same boat.

Acknowledged first in 1951 for its scientific interest; Hothfield common as an unusual assortment of wildlife, rare plants and insect life. In February 2008, Hothfield Common was renamed, Hothfield Heathland Nature Reserve. The Common is two hundred acres of grassland, bogs and bracken covered woods, and is one of the last of its kind remaining in Kent. In the past, residents of Hothfield harvested the common for its timber, peat moss, heather and bracken; at one time, they even grazed their livestock there. Snuggled in the Weald of Kent between the North and South Downs; Hothfield Common is surrounded by dairy farms, wheat fields, orchards, and hop fields.

During the Second World War, there were over four hundred Nissan huts built on the common to accommodate army personnel. The army also took over Hothfield Place Mansion in 1939 and used it as Headquarters for a British Army Battalion and the Home Guard. In June of 1944, a V-1 flying bomb *(doodlebug)* badly damaged the Mansion as well as the bell tower of St Margaret's Church. Giant cypress trees to the south of the church took the brunt of the V1's blast. Split apart by the force of the explosion, the trees were later pulled back together, and to my knowledge are still standing with the chains embedded deep inside the trunks. In a four-month period that same year, the Germans launched over 9000 of these flying bombs from locations in France and Belgium. Approximately 2500 of these V-1's hit London. V-1's, with their rudimentary guidance system and a warhead filled with 1800 pounds of high explosives were filled with just enough fuel to reach London. Some V-1s, running low on fuel, fell short over the county of Kent, randomly hitting the ground and exploding, earning Kent County the nickname, *Bomb Alley*. Eight of these doodlebugs fell in the Parish of

Hothfield, blowing out windows and fraying nerves of many residents. Fortunately, there were no deaths recorded. Anti-aircraft guns, R.A.F. fighter planes and barrage balloons brought down others. After the war, the army returned the Mansion to Lord Hothfield. He eventually sold it to Sir Reginald Roots, who then built a new brick mansion there in 1954 and had the war torn mansion demolished.

With a shortage of places to live in post war England, the Ashford District Council began using the vacant army huts on the common to house families. Although Hothfield was a picturesque little village, Hothfield Hut Camp had a reputation as a deprived area with rundown living conditions. We had passed by the Hut Camp many times on the bus when traveling between Charing and Ashford. My mother never giving it a second thought as a place to live.

As we drove out of Ashford, the man from the housing office informed my mother that we were going to Hothfield Hut Camp. One of these ex-army huts would now become our new home. After a fifteen-minute drive, we turned off the main road onto a dirt trail, stopping outside one of these Nissan huts. Taking a set of keys from his briefcase, the man reached back from the front seat and handed them to my mother, he then advised her that she would need a shilling for the electric meter. As we exited the car, he bade us a dutiful goodnight and drove off, no doubt glad to be out of an awkward situation that had plagued him all that day.

Groping in the evening light, my mother found the keyhole and unlocked the door. A loud creak from rusty door hinges was a good indication nobody had been living there for a while. Inside, the odour of musty stale air permeated the place. It was obvious too, with one of the windows left ajar and the rubbish left lying around that squatters had spent some time there. The floor also showed signs of a mice infestation. Putting the suitcase down, my mother took a slow walk through the place. The hut, made up of three separate rooms, had a half round corrugated roof supported by a rough cement floor. The cheap, whitewashed wallboard lining the walls had warped from the cold and damp. The rusty metal windows were draughty and covered in dusty cobwebs. The front room was both the kitchen and living area. The sink had a single tap with cold running water. The coal fireplace had an open grate with an attached side oven and sat in the middle of the room against the inside wall. The center room was dark and windowless, a bare light fixture hung from the ceiling. This would be our bedroom, as it was close to the living room and picked up some warmth from the fireplace. The backroom with its two small windows was damp and musty, and used mostly as a playroom. A small shed outside housed our toilet. It had a large metal bucket with a wooden seat; tattered newspaper littered the floor. The bucket, when full, would need empting at a central septic pit. The shed also doubled as a coal storage area.

Coming back inside to the front room, my mother sat down on the suitcase and propped herself up against the wall. With the cold of the evening starting to draw in, my sister and I huddled in close beside her. Tired and stressed out from a long day spent at the housing office, my mother was thankful, finally to have a roof over our heads.

Sitting there in the muted evening light of the hut, her thoughts now turned towards something to eat. While checking her purse for a shilling to put in the electric meter, there was a soft knock at the door. Before my mother could get up to answer it, the door slowly opened. Looking up, she was startled to see the silhouette of a man's face coming through the door. Moving quickly to her feet, she nervously ordered him to stop and state his business. "Don't be alarmed mam," he said, "My names Tom Buss. I live in the hut just across the way. I saw you arrive and I couldn't help noticing you have no furniture. Is everything alright?" Emotionally drained by now and close to tears, my mother told him that she had no furniture, "nothing, not a thing!"

Giving her a warm smile, he said, "Come with me I think I can help you, I'll get my wife to make you a cup of tea for a start." Taking us across to his hut, he introduced us to his two daughters, Rosemary, Theresa, and wife Tear. My mother introduced herself, Karen and me. Over cups of tea and fried egg sandwiches, my mother explained her situation to them: how she had lost her job at "Hillside Farm" in Tumbridge Wells and how we had spent the winter in an old bus at Monkery Bottom, then our move to Charing, where she had worked "In Service" for a Colonel Dagueneau and his family. My mother told them about the difficulties that had arisen over the disciplining of Karen and John, by the Colonel and the supervision of the Dagueneaus daughter's affairs by my mother. Put out of the house with one day's notice. How we had spent the day in Ashford at the housing commission office, filling out forms and doing interviews in order to find a place to live. Apparently, all available housing was for married couples with two or more children, leaving the Salvation Army as the only choice for someone in my mother's situation. When it was time for the office to close, she explained how she had refused to go to the Army Hostel or leave the office until they found us a place to live. Not wanting to cause a scene, the housing commission finally relented and gave us one of the huts.

After giving my mother a sympathetic ear, Tom excused

himself. Leaving his place with a bucket, broom and scrub brush, he told my mother not to worry about a thing; we were to stay with his wife and he would be back in awhile. Returning a short time later, he took us back across to our hut. Here we found the hut cleaned and the trash left by squatters gone, and a fire going in the grate. Tom, who was somewhat of a patriarch in the hut camp community, put out the word that a family was in need and could anyone help. Shortly, people were coming and going, bringing in bits and pieces of furniture, food, pots and pans and coal. They were kind-hearted people who had very little themselves, helping out in any way they could, with what ever they could spare. As folk left, my mother, overcome by their kindness, thanked each one of them. An outpouring of kindness she was very grateful for and never forgot.

Tom returned a short time later to see how we were settling in. He mentioned to my mother that he worked as a maintenance man at Lenham Sanatorium. Perched high on the side of the North Downs, Lenham Sanatorium was a medical facility for long term care of tuberculosis patients. If she were interested, he would keep an eye out as to any job openings that might suit her. My mother told him she would be grateful and willing to take anything that was available. She thanked Tom again for all he and his wife had done. She then asked him if he knew of someone who might be able to pick up the pedal car and scooter, which we had left behind at Dagueneaus' in Charing. He told my mother he would arrange to have them picked up some time in the next few days. With the hut now warming up, my mother made-up our bed and we climbed into it, thankful for the day's mercies.

The next morning we woke early and my mother lit a fire,

put the kettle on for tea, and made a pot of oatmeal. After breakfast, she called on Tear to see if there was a grocery store near by. She told my mother there was a small shop at the top of Tutt Hill called, "Willis's." Here she purchased a few groceries, cleaning supplies and the proverbial mousetraps. Back at the hut, she gave the place another good cleaning, and strategically placed the mousetraps, one in each room.

The following week, my mother took Karen and me down to the village of Hothfield to register for school. Built in 1874 by Sir Henry Tufton, the school was located on the corner of Hothfield Common. The school had three main classrooms; attached to each classroom was a small cloakroom with a washbasin. An open coal fireplace in the central classroom heated the school and warmed our cold hands and feet on winter days. The toilets were outside at the back of the school, and on the roof was a small steeple that housed a bell to summon children to class. The dirt playground had four or five large fir trees growing in the yard. In a game of tag, the trees were considered home base. At the back of the playground, there was a large concrete air raid shelter built during World War II. Outside the school fence was the village green that doubled as a playing field. At the far end of the playing field, near the crossroads of Cade and Station Road was another large concrete pillbox, it was demolished in the late fifties.

The Head Mistress, Miss Bottle, made us very welcome. The school catered mostly to Hothfield children, ranging in age from five to eleven years old, with a kindergarten class in the village hall. Some students came from Little Chart and Pluckley. Every morning at recess, there was a small bottle of cool refreshing milk for each student; for some children this would be their breakfast. At noon, a canteen van would arrive at school with hot dinners. It cost my mother five shillings a week for my sister and me to have a hot meal at lunchtime. Some children did not care for the mobile meals, so they brought sandwiches from home instead. Myself, I had no complaints!

At that time, there was no library at Hothfield School, so once a month a large dark blue library van would make its way around to rural schools. This gave children the opportunity to access books to help with their schoolwork. We could choose three books per visit as long as one of the books related to our schoolwork. It was obvious by the graffiti scrawled in the dust on the side of the van that it had been to other schools. One of Miss Bottle's strictest rules was that when the library van came to Hothfield School, no students were to go anywhere near it until it was their turn to get books. She was very proud of the fact that none of her students ever defaced the vehicle.

With the school situated on the common, Miss Bottle had another strict rule. No students were allowed to go anywhere near the bogs at recess. Like fleas to a dog, the boys couldn't stay away from the swamps. In the spring, it was a great place to hunt for frogs, slow worms, and newts. There were many times, while in the pursuit of some aquatic trophy, the school bell would ring and in a mad dash to get back to class, students would occasionally end up with a wet foot or two. This meant you had to sit through afternoon classes with soggy feet. There were times when the teacher would ask the rhetorical question, "Has anyone been playing in the bogs at recess?" No one would ever admit to it, but the puddles under some desks were a dead giveaway.

As far as discipline went, there was not any kind of corporal punishment on Miss Bottle's watch, although that did change when Mr. Purkis became Headmaster. Mrs. Shersby, the music teacher, was a very kind and caring person, but firm. She had a piano in the corner of her room. Any misbehaviour and students would find themselves standing behind it for five or ten minutes, depending on the severity of the behaviour. She also had a large jar of sweets standing on her desk. This was a reminder to students that, if they had not been sent behind the piano more than once that week, they could choose something from out of the jar at the end of the week. Every Friday afternoon, just before dismissal, Mrs. Shersby would come around with the sweet jar, giving what seemed to be a core group of boys a miss each week. Many times, she would give me a pass too, saying, "Now John, I don't like to do this, but you must try harder next week to be good." This was of very little comfort to me, as the other kids sat at their desks smacking on large gob-stopper. On the outside, I was very nonchalant, but on the inside, I was green with envy. After school on Friday's, we would drift home in groups of have and have-nots. Kids deprived of the sweet jar, commiserated with one another about the unfairness of Mrs. Shersby and her jar of sweets.

On the other hand, Miss Bottle's discipline came in the form of a good telling-off if students were disobedient. Embarrassing the pupil in front of the whole class, with her high-pitched voice, she would let everyone know all about their latest blunder. If a student had been particularly unruly, she would grab them by the shoulders and give them a good hard shake and in doing so, try to shake some sense into them, I suppose! Miss Bottle, being an unmarried woman the older kids interpreted this back and forth shaking motion of boys as her way of "getting her jollies." I went through a number of these up-close and personal encounters with Miss

Bottle while at Hothfield Primary. One time, she had caught me flicking a bar of soap around the cloakroom and a few times for playing in the bogs. Another time while playing a game of "it", some of the girls had complained to Miss Bottle that the boys kept tagging them on the chest. Whilst she was shaking you back and forth, the older boys chuckled away and mimicked her actions behind her back. All the while, you were trying to keep a straight face as you endured one of these head-jarring experiences.

The A20 was the major road in the fifties. Running from London to Dover and passing right through Hothfield Hut Camp. With no speed limits on the highways in those days, it made the road a very dangerous place to be. The fact that I was unable to pedal my car on the dirt paths of the common made this stretch of road an ideal surface for me to pedal on. Pushing the car out into the road one day, I jumped in and began to pump the pedals as fast as my legs would go. As cars and lorries sped by me honking their horns, I never gave them a second thought; quite happy to think I was one of them. It was not long however, before a police car arrived on the scene.

Jumping out of his car, the police officer grabbed me by the scruff of the neck and snatched me out of my little car. With his other hand, he took the pedal car and threw it into the ditch. He then marched me home to my mother, where he chastised her for allowing me to be out on the main road with a pedal car. No doubt embarrassed by the situation, she gave me a good hiding and sent me to the back room of the hut for the rest of the afternoon. Following that incident, my mother only allowed me to have the pedal car on the pathway up to Willis's whenever she went shopping.

A few weeks after my mother had dealt with the pedal

car incident, I was amusing myself outside when some older boys came along. One of them suggested we go out to the main road and throw stones at cars. I'm not sure if it was peer pressure at the time, or it just sounded like fun, but off we went out to the road. On the way, we found a large piece of chain in another kid's yard and decided it might be a good thing to drag out into the road and watch cars thump over it. After bouncing pebbles off a few cars with no reaction, we decided it was time for the chain. As I was the youngest and maybe the most gullible, they picked me to pull the chain out to the middle of the road. With a break in the traffic, I grabbed one end and away I went dragging all four feet of it into the center of the road. Glancing up at the sound of an approaching car, I saw, much to my horror a police car coming toward me. Looking around for some support, or a chance to play the blame game, I saw my three fellow cohorts high tailing it down the pathway and disappearing. As the police car swung to the curb, a very angry looking officer jumped out of the car and came toward me. By the time I had got to the side of the road and decided to make a run for it, a heavy hand caught me by the collar and I was again, high-stepped all the way back to my mother. Only this time I knew what the penalty would be. No amount of pleading or protesting would diminish my punishment. Another good hiding and into the backroom I went for one more long afternoon of sombre reflection.

At my young age, I'm sure my mother thought she was dealing with a six-year-old delinquent. By now, she had had enough of police officers and notes home from school and decided it was time to nip things in the bud. I had already been in the back room for a couple of hours when my mother came in with my sister. She sat us both down for a good long talk. "Your mum," she said "is a single parent. I'm trying hard to make a home and a good life for you and Karen. Everything you do reflects on your mother, the good, and the bad. Every time you get into trouble, or make a nuisance of yourself, people will say that is what becomes of having no father in the home. You don't want people saying your mum's not a good mother, do you?" It was such an emotional talk, that at my young age, it touched me somewhere deep inside and I never forgot it. I'm not saying I was a perfect kid after that talk, but it did cross my mind a few times when it looked as if trouble might be coming my way.

The first couple of weeks in Hothfield had been a little stressful on my mother as we began to settle in and she looked for work. Tom, however, did have a little good news for her one day. A job opening had come up at the Sanatorium for a domestic; he had gone ahead and made an appointment for my mother to have an interview that coming Friday.

Friday morning, Karen and I got ready for school, while my mother prepared to go to Lenham Sanatorium for her job interview. When we returned home from school that afternoon, we found my mum in high spirits. She had been hired on at the sanatorium and would start work the following Monday. This meant she would have to catch a bus at seven in the morning, returning home after five in the afternoon, leaving Karen and me to get ourselves off to school in the morning, and to cross the busy A20 main road. One of my mother's major concerns was about where we lived relative to the school. A few of the other families knew of her concerns about our being left alone and kindly stepped in to keep an eye on us. There were many times I fell asleep in Tom's home after school and woke up in my own home, unaware that he had carried me back to our hut when my mum came home.

That's the way people were, they shared, cared and watched out for each other, making sure kids were safe.

Mrs. Housdan eventually caught up with us after our quick departure from Dagueneaus in Charing. My mother told her that she was working at Lenham Sanatorium and was happy with her situation in Hothfield. She did however mention to Mrs. Housdan, her concern about Karen and me having to cross the A20 to get to school and back home each day. If there were any way she could help assist us in a move to the south side, it would ease some of my mother's fears of leaving us during the day. Mrs. Housdan said she would put an application into the housing council, requesting a move to the south side for us. She also told my mother that their records indicated that Simon was back in England and working up in Essex; paper work had been set in motion and she would soon be able to collect alimony. My mother had concerns as to whether or not Simon would request visitation rights for Karen and me but he never did. She also told my mother that a family in South Africa had set up a benevolent fund; its purpose was to help families in England who might be in need after the war. This came in the form of ten-pounds just before the school started each year. This helped my mum out immensely with the purchase of school uniforms and clothes for the school year. Mrs. Housdan also told my mother that plans for the new housing estate at Hothfield were well under way. The council was looking at vacant land opposite the school for the project. They should start the logging process sometime in the next couple of years. Families living on the common would get first pick of the new council houses. They would then demolish the huts and return the common to its natural state. The thought of a new house to live in was a little to much for my mother to comprehend, having fought hard just to get into one of the huts. Other families on the camp dismissed it as just a rumour. They had heard it all before.

A few months later, with the request for our move to the south side granted, we moved to hut number 615 Cade Road. Here my mother felt more settled and began to make us a home in the hut, just as she had done with the old bus at Monkery Bottom. The first couple of months there was paint and paper on the walls, new curtains on the windows and linoleum on the floors. A house is not a home without a cat, and with that thought in mind, one day my mother brought home a little kitten and we named it Whiskers.

Station Road was the main road into Hothfield Village for most commercial vehicles and buses. Cade Road was the secondary route. Here kids could play without too much fear of traffic. It was like having our own paved playground right outside our hut and with the postwar baby boom, there was no shortage of kids to play with.

My mother always left for work right after breakfast at around seven and returned home at five. As we got older, she had a number of chores my sister and I would need to have done before she came home. Morning breakfast dishes washed, table laid and potatoes peeled for our evening meal. Floor swept, coal brought in from the shed and the fire lit. Each week my mother would make her legendary old fashion bread-pudding for my sister and me to snack on after school. Any kids willing to help with our chores knew their reward would be a slice of this scrumptious delicacy. At the end of the week, for chores well done, our mother would bring Karen and me home a large bar of *"Sharps Toffee,"* from Charing.

School was now about a one-mile walk from where we lived. There were no school buses in those days, so no matter how foul the weather, we always made the best of it. A game of ball tag or leapfrog would help make the hike a little more interesting. In September, Hothfield Common would start to come alive with all its fall colors. Giant oak, chestnut and beech trees with their many shades of green would slowly progress into hues of gold, bronze and amber. Valleys and dales of green bracken turned into a carpet of golden brown. Wild holly, rose hips, mistletoe and ivy would soon be ready for Christmas wreaths. Crunching through the mounds of dry fall leaves, we would kick up chestnuts that had fallen from the trees. These always made a tasty little snack on the way to and from school. Huge horse chestnut trees with their bounty of conkers were a big fad in the fall. Boys, in a game of conkers, would try all kinds of tricks to harden their conkers to knock out the competition.

Soon the pleasant days of fall would give way to the chilly winds of winter. Blowing off the North Sea, these winds brought with them the freezing rain, sleet and sometimes snow. It was a teeth chattering time of year to be walking to school, but sliding on frozen puddles helped break the dreariness of the trek. On cold frosty mornings when the air was crisp and clear, our hot breath would hit the cold air in a plume of pseudo smoke. Acting all sophisticated, we would often pretend we were smoking a cigarette. Some days, a rare snowfall would be a chance to slide down the slippery slopes of the dales on a sheet of cardboard or tin, or we would fling ourselves into a snowball fight. These activities would occasionally make us late for school. On these mornings, it was always tempting to cut across the frozen bog, to get to school. There were times though, when the ice would not be thick enough to carry your weight and we would end up with a frozen wet foot or two. At times like these, we were thankful for the big open coal fireplace at school where we could hang our socks and shoes to dry.

Although television sets were starting to become available, no one in the huts we knew had one. Throughout the long winter nights, we spent most of our time listening to the radio, or playing board games; *Snakes and Ladders, Tidily Winks,* or *Ludo,* were just a few we enjoyed. Our mum would pass the time darning socks, or knitting balaclavas and gloves to help ward off the winter chills. She also liked to pass the time studying her Football Pools, spending many hours in the evening pouring over the sports pages and picking out her favourites teams. Choosing a line-up of eight games she thought would end in draws was her favourite pursuit. On the weekend, she would listen intently to the radio as the announcer read out the results. Checking them off to see how her line-up had fared, there would often be a mumbled cuss or two. This indicated to Karen and me that we would not be moving to our new mansion any time soon. There was only one time I ever remember our mum winning anything significant. It was about fifty pounds, almost three months wages for her in those days.

Spring would start to show itself with the appearance of house sparrows, chattering away as they went about building their nest in the eaves of huts. The melodic songs of the thrush, robin and blackbird, or the distant call of the cuckoo, would cheer us on our walk to school. Milk bottles filled with pussy willows, cattails and wildflowers, picked by students on the way to school, adorned the windowsills of classrooms. The Downs, with its sea of blue bells, was another sure sign that spring had arrived. With the coming of spring, children would start to show up on the street once again and the popularity of games would start all over. One week it might be hopscotch, with one or two games scratched out on the road. Another week, it could be five stones. The game would test your skill and quickness at throwing five stones in the air and catching them on the back of your hand, while performing certain tasks. A great deal of time would be spent picking out just the right stones. Hoop was another popular pass-time for boys. Contests were set up and old bike wheels became our imaginary race cars, bowling them around an obstacle course laid out on the road. There was always a game or two of marbles going on with the boys as well. Girls liked to skip rope and sing out their little ditties, *"I like coffee, I like tea, I like Johnny, and he likes me,"* or replace the name with any other boy they could embarrass that happened to be in range of their voices. Experienced skippers with a long rope would have two or three girls join in at the same time. Single skippers, too, had their own set of skills, jumping high enough to skip the rope two or three times: backwards skip, cross arm skip, or skipping two together. Yo-yos would be another way we would pass the time, trying hard to learn all the tricks, but most of the time we were happy just to get the spool to go up and down. One summer, the American phenomenon of the Hula-Hoop made an appearance and was all the rage. There was only one thing I remember that would stop all the playfulness on the street for fifteen minutes each day, "The Archers." The program came on the radio from quarter to seven till seven in the evening. Stories of farming, romance, and relationships, even murder, all covered in this, *"Every day story of country folk."* Back out on the street fifteen-minute later the saga would be the subject of much debate and speculation until the next episode. Squash Beans, Kick-the-Can and Hide-and-Seek were all games we played in large groups. The more the merrier and with a two hundred acre common to hide in, games could last until dark. Knock out Ginger, was one of our more mischievous games we played. I'm not sure why we got so much pleasure out of knocking on people's doors and running away, but we did.

Summer days the common became our theatre to act out many of our childhood fantasies. Robin Hood, Ivanhoe and Roy Rogers, were but a few. On weekends, with the wide open spaces of the common, we would ride the range all day, until teatime. One day while out playing Cowboys and Indians, we decided that our smoke signals would be more authentic if we had a real fire. With that in mind, I took a box of matches and a blanket along next time and we got a small fire going. While waving the blanket over the smoke, it caught on fire. In an attempt to put out the flaming blanket, I threw it on the ground and we began to stomp on it. Before we knew it, fire spread to some dry bracken and soon we were out of our depth with a brush fire. In a panic, we were onto our pretend horses and riding away as fast as our legs would go. Across the bog and up to Foxenhill Toll we rode. There we watched as the fire blazed away, creeping ever closer to some of the huts. Before long though there was the sound of a fire engine bell and the Charing Fire Brigade were on scene to put out the blaze. After hiding out for a couple of hours during all the excitement, we finally skulked back home. Conspicuous by our absence, we found it hard to convince people we had nothing to do with the fire.

The back yard of our hut was another popular place on the street. It had a large sandy area that was a great place for kids to play in with their toys. It was also a well-visited area by all the neighbourhood cats. At times, this made digging and playing in the sand a sticky stinky place to be at times, although, I'm sure it helped us build up a strong immune systems.

Another notable sight at the bottom of our yard was a tall fir tree; many times kids had attempted to climb it. A few times some made it halfway up, lost their nerve and came back down. One day, my sister Karen casually declared that she was going to climb the tree. Nobody took her comment seriously at the time and we all carried on digging in the dirt. It was not until my mother came out of the hut and inquired as to who was up the tree did we realize that Karen had made it all the way to the top. I said to my mum "I think its Karen." Looking up, all you could see was her dress waving in the breeze. My mother's first reaction was to start hollering at her to get back down, then with a cooler head prevailing; she began to coax her down. Gathering around the bottom of the tree, kids, in a sort of hero worship watched as Karen started her decent. That was the first and last time we ever saw anyone climb that tree.

My pedal car was the only one in the neighbourhood and the centre of much attention. Tired of pedalling the car, we found it could go much faster with a couple of kids pulling you. Tying a piece of rope to the front bumper, we took turns running from one end of the street to the other as fast as we could go with a kid in tow. It was on one of these particular days that one of the older boys from the camp come riding towards us on a rickety old bike – a bike no less. No kids on the camp we knew had a bike; only a few of the working people had one. Questioning him as to where he got it, he told us that he had put it together up at Ashford dump. The Norman Bicycle Company in Ashford used the dump to discard old parts and pieces, along with other people's old bikes. With a few spanners, a puncture kit, and a little ingenuity, you could put a bike together in a few hours. The following Saturday, with tools in hand, Michael Tamsett and I walked the four miles to the dump. After a couple of hours scrounging around, dodging rats and the caretaker, we managed to put a couple of mock-up bikes together and ride home. I did not exactly ride home. The front wheel of my bike was half the size of the back wheel and I was unable to find a bike-chain, so I found myself scooting the bike home. Mike had fared a little better and managed to ride home. After a few more trips to the dump, I finally got all the bits and pieces to fit and I had my first bike.

There were only three things on my wish list when I was young that I really wanted. One was a new bike, a fishing rod and rubber wheeled roller skates. My mother's standard answer to all this wishing was, *"if wishes were horses, beggars would ride."* This answer always irritated my sister and me when we were in our wishing mode. Karen had always wanted roller skates and a new bike too. Things never came easy for us, my mother being a single parent. True to her word though, if she said next Christmas or wait for your birthday, she would always do her best to fulfill the promises.

For now though, an article in the newspaper had sparked her interest. Ashford council were going to start logging land opposite the school in Hothfield in preparation for the new housing estate. With that in mind, my mother's thoughts now turned toward furniture in hopes of moving to one of the new houses. Skates and bikes would have to take a back seat. My mother did however make me a promise though; she told me that when I finally did get my bike, it would be the best bike in the village.

Chapter 9

#7 Common Way

*My mother found a great deal of satisfaction
working with the elderly and infirm, that she
made geriatrics her life long occupation.*

In the 1950's, with WW II behind her, England began to move into a more prosperous era. A prosperity that had been hard fought for and won by the sacrifices of many men and women in two world wars. With cease-fire talks ongoing with North Korea and signs of a peace agreement with Egypt over the Suez Canal, England was now moving into the fifties in relative peace. Although, there was still rationing in effect on some foods and luxury items, we were too young at the time to understand the significance of this scarcity.

Housing families displaced by the war was part of the government's plan as they began logging the land opposite Hothfield School in 1952. Throughout the summer, families from the huts gathered on the village green to watch as the giant oak, beech and chestnut trees came down. Logs were then loaded onto large timber-tugs and hauled away to the mills. Stumps, some four feet in diameter, with there enormous root systems, had to be blown out of the ground with dynamite in order to remove them. In the evening, we would gather up the wood-chips left behind from the logging for firewood; this would help supplement our heating bills.

Soon, the new roads began to take shape and houses started to go up. After school, we would wander around the building site, choosing where we would like to live, hopeful that our friends would be living close by. For my mother, one of these new houses would be a dream come true, but she did not let her hopes get too high. As a single parent, she had had a real struggle just to get into one of the huts. Now, having worked hard to make a comfortable home for us there, we were happy just to be living on the hut camp.

At the time, there was also a move afoot by the government to get gypsy families off the roads and into permanent housing. With a number of them spending more and more time camped on the common and with poor sanitary conditions, it started to affect the ecology of Hothfield Common. Rumours suggested that with the increased number of them camped there; Hothfield is where the government would start implementing the plan as soon as the new houses were finished. This raised concern with the hut dwellers as to just how many of them would actually get to move into the new houses. Some, who had lived in the huts since the end of W.W.II thought they should have first consideration.

By the summer of 1954, resident of the huts started to receive letters informing them of a move to the new estate. John and Clare Nicholls were the first to get their keys to a new house, setting up home in School Road. This quashed rumours that gypsies would get the first pick. Delighted by this news, my mother now believed it might just be possible she would get one of these new houses. A house she had dreamt about and desired since deciding to stay in Kent rather than going back to London. Trips into Ashford now took on a more urgent nature, as she began to look for new furniture. The first thing on her list was a living-room suite. A dark burgundy sofa and chair had caught her eye, and with a small down payment on the *H.P.* plan, she began to pay them off each week.

It was about a month later that my mother received the keys to her new council house. Number 7 Common Way would be our address. With a great deal of excitement, we ran down the road to have a look at what would be our new home. When we arrived at the house, there was a party going on in Number 5 Common Way, much to our surprise. It was the one-hundredth council house to be finished and they were using Number 7 for food preparation. When my mother asked if we could go in and have a look around, one of the council representatives told her she would have to come back tomorrow. It was a bit of a let down, but she was able to tell us that the house was a three-bedroom with indoor bathroom, lavatory and living room. The kitchen was equipped with a Rayburn cooker that would also supply us with hot water. This would be our first home with the luxury of hot running water, indoor plumbing and a bedroom of our own.

Back home at the hut, my mother made plans to have our furniture moved the following weekend. In a melancholy mood, we began to pack boxes in anticipation of the move. Although happy to have a new home to live in, we were sad to be leaving our hut. It was the first place we had settled for any length of time and my mother had made a comfortable home for us there. Living in the huts at that time everyone was in the same boat. We all got along with one another and there were no pretences amongst us. A cup of sugar here, scoops of coal there, or a couple of cigarettes borrowed one week, were paid back the following week. My mother only had one little extravagance besides her cigarettes and that was the daily newspaper. Apart from the news and crossword puzzle, she liked to keep track of her football teams. After picking out her line-up and placing a little bet for the weekend, she would pass the papers on to the neighbours. These would sometimes end up as a tablecloth for some or toilet paper for others. A move now to the new estate would mean making new friends and neighbours.

On the day of the move, there was no shortage of folks willing to give a helping hand. Neighbours introduced themselves as they helped carry boxes and furniture into our new home, while the women made pots of tea. Settling into our new home Karen and I put dibs on which bedroom we would have and who would be the first to bathe in the new bathtub. It was not long before my mother finished paying off her living room suite and sideboard and went in for new bedroom furniture. Curtains for the windows and carpets for the floors and stairs would soon follow.

Common Way is a small pathway cutting through a corner of the estate between Coach Drive and School Road. It was a pleasant neighbourhood with most of our friends living close by. The homes were a combination of two-story, semi-detached and row houses built of brick on either side of the pathway. This style of housing was popping up like mushrooms all over post war England. Number 7 was situated in the hollow of Common Way and that first winter, when the heavy rains came, we found ourselves in the middle of a flood. However, after adding extra drainage to our front garden, the problem was finally alleviated.

Along with a move to the new house, a job opening came up at Hothfield Hospital for a nursing aid. The institution catered mainly to the elderly. My mother put in her application and was lucky enough to get the job a week later. The hospital was only a one-mile walk across the common from our house, giving her an opportunity to spend more time at home. She found a great deal of satisfaction working at Hothfield Hospital, and with much empathy and compassion for the elderly, my mother made geriatric care her life long occupation.

Soon Common Way became one of the more attractive areas on the estate. Mrs. Jamison, who lived just across from us, won best garden three years in a row for her beautiful roses. The Butler girls dug a sunken flower garden in their front yard. Mr. Sharman made an attractive little gate for his front yard and before he knew it, he had more orders for gates than he could handle. Flowers, lawns and shrubs went into other yards making Common Way a pleasant and attractive place to live. Unfortunately, other areas of Hothfield estate did not fare so well.

With a number of gypsy families approved to move into the new houses on the estate, they brought with them many of their gypsy ways. Most of them settled in well to the more domestic way of life and added a cultural flavour to the village. Some families did not fair so well in this more permanent way of life and went back on the road again. Others, with little regard for their neighbourhoods, allowed their houses to fall into disrepair. Inside their homes, doors, cupboards and counters, anything they could burn, they chopped up and used as firewood. Broken windows and yards piled up with scrap metal did not sit well with neighbours. This resulted in some evictions and left Hothfield Village, again, with a reputation as not a very desirable place to live.

While out playing one day, one of their mangy gyppo dogs bit me on the backside. When my mother confronted the owner of the dog, she was harassed and verbally assaulted. The dog was eventually euthanized, leaving a simmering hostility towards us on the part of the dog owner. The older gyppo kids bullied the younger children too, nicking their toys and sweets, or any other thing that might take their fancy.

With all this in mind and the approach of the summer school break, my mother did not like the idea of Karen and me staying around Hothfield for six weeks by ourselves, while she was at work. She expressed her concerns to Mrs. Housdan, who suggested to my mother that there were families willing to look after children in her situation for the summer holidays. If my mother was interested, Mrs. Housdan said she would make some inquires for her.

Before we new it, Karen and I were off to Dymchurch for the summer, a small picturesque, seaside town on the south coast of Kent. The idea of spending a month at the seaside did sound appealing to us. However, upon arrival, we found that Mr. and Mrs. Remple were an older couple and a little on the frail side. They had little interest in going to the beach and depended mostly on their teenage son, an only child, to do the shopping and run errands for them. There were times when their son took great pleasure in teasing my sister unmercifully. Because of the difficulty of getting to Dymchurch from Hothfield by bus, my mum was not able to visit us regularly. At one point, Karen and I made plans to run away, but never quite got up the nerve. At the end of the summer, glad to be back in Hothfield, we told our mother we never wanted to go back to Dymchurch again. During the summer, my mum had taken on some additional work and with the extra money, surprised us with new carpeting for the living room.

Since Dymchurch had been our first summer away from home and been a big disappointment, Mrs. Housdan was confident the following year would be different. She found us a new family to stay with at Challock. It was a little closer to Hothfield, with two children the same age as Karen and I, which Mrs. Housdan thought, should make things a little easier for us. Unfortunately, the father turned out to be a firm disciplinarian, something Karen and I were not used to, particularly coming from a man. Again, we were not happy and made plans to run away back home to Hothfield.

However, the plan was cut short one day while we were out playing. Walking down to the corner shop for sweets, we stopped to watch a farmer fixing a mower that had broken down. As the men worked on the piece of equipment, I, along with two other boys, climbed up on the tractor and took turns pretending to drive it. Taking a little more time than I should have with my turn, a shoving match ensued resulting in my falling backwards off the tractor toward the engine. With my right arm caught between the engine and the steering bar, I fell backwards, fracturing my elbow. When I came too, I was lying on my back under the tractor. I heard one of the farmhands say, "I think he's broke his arm." Unable to move and going in and out of consciousness, I feared I was dying, peed my pants and passed out again. I am not sure how long I lay there, but the sound of a bell stirred me. One of farmhands helped me to my feet and we walked across the field toward a waiting ambulance, my right arm-hanging limp by my side. In the ambulance, the only thing I remember was the attendant asking me my name. I do not recall another thing until I woke up in the hospital the next day with my mum sitting beside my bed.

This put a painful, but thankful end to our Challock summer. After a week in the hospital, I returned home to Hothfield. My mother had been busy over the summer and had another surprise for us. She had purchased a new bedroom suite for me.

For Karen and me, Challock had been the last straw. "No more summer holidays away from home," we told our mother. As we were getting older, my mother began to see our side of things. "Well, you have a year to think about it," she said. "Maybe you'll change your mind by next summer." Mrs. Housdan knew of Karen and my opposition to these holidays and made us a promise. She would find us a more compatible family next year.

Back at school that fall, with a fractured right elbow and a cast from my shoulder to the fingertips I struggled to get my schoolwork done. After a few difficulties with the elbow not setting right, it finally came together and I got the cast off six months later.

As fall passed into winter and winter into spring, the summer holidays debate loomed once again. Mrs. Housdan mentioned to my mother that she had found a young couple who lived on a farm, just outside Pluckley. They had no children of their own at the time, but were willing to have us spend the summer holidays with them. After much protest, Karen and I agreed to go meet the Sages, on the understanding that if we were not happy we could come home.

The fact that the Sages lived on a farm did have some appeal to me, even though I had broken my arm on a tractor the year before. Leaving Hothfield with an uneasy feeling, our bags packed for only a two-week stay at the farm. My mum joked as we drove off "Who knows, maybe third time lucky." As Pluckley was only five miles from Hothfield, we told our mum it was not too far to walk home if we were not happy. Pluckley was also on a scheduled bus route; so my mum assured us she would visit us every Saturday and bring us some pocket money.

Arriving at the village of Pluckley, Mrs. Housdan made a sharp right turn down a small country lane past green fields and orchards toward Pevington Farm. The Sages lived in small semi-detached flint-stone cottage, set back in a corner of the farmyard. This tranquil little cottage had a flower filled front garden, ablaze with a rich array of roses, dahlias, lupines and hollyhocks. At the back of the house was a large vegetable plot, with a young attractive woman working the ground. Despite my young age, she caught my eye and I was happy to find out that this was Mrs. Sage. Exciting the car, the ambiance of the farmyard filled the air. The aroma of new mown hay piled high in a barn, rolling green fields, apple orchards, and chickens scratching in the yard. For a moment, my thoughts flashed back to the time we had lived at Hillside Farm near Tunbridge Wells.

As we entered the garden, Mrs. Sage called out to her husband, "Alan." He was in a shed at the back of the garden tinkering with an old motorcycle. Mr. Sage was a good-looking man, black wavy hair, a twinkle in his eye and a ready smile. His face and arms, tanned from long days spent working in the fields. After the introductions, Mrs. Sage took us into the farmhouse for tea. Inside the house, there was a wonderful aroma of baking. In anticipation of our visit, Mrs Sage had baked a "Gypsy Tart."

Over tea, the Sages engaged Karen and me in conversation. "For starters," said Mrs. Sage, "If you are going to stay with us for a while, I'm your Aunt Margaret and this is your Uncle Alan, okay!" This surprised me somewhat; at all the other summer homes it had been mister and missus. She then asked as to our likes and dislikes, what kinds of foods we were fond of, games we liked to play, and if we liked animals.

Following tea, we went outside where Aunt Margaret showed us her vegetable garden, filled with runner beans, carrots, beetroot, potatoes and a large rhubarb patch. In a back shed, there were a number of hutches with her much-loved brood of guinea pigs. Uncle Alan then took us on a tour of the farmyard. There were so many barns, out buildings and lofts. Uncle Alan suggested it was a great place to play hide and seek or kick the can in the evenings. In one of the barns was a big old sow with a litter of piglets. One was a little runt. Aunt Margaret had taken the little one under her wing and was bottle-feeding it. Another barn filled with bales of straw looked like a great place to build a fort.

At the end of the long driveway was Mr. Muier's house, the landowner. Here we met Peggy, his housekeeper and her son Michael, who became one of our good friends. By now, it was getting late in the afternoon, and on the way back to the cottage my mum needed to know if we were going to stay. It was clear to my sister and me that the Sage's were a devoted and fun loving couple, who would really enjoy having us stay with them for the summer. I do not remember there being much of a question as to whether we would stay. In that short time, Karen and I had both felt a special bond with the Sages and decided to spend the summer with them. We, were excited too about living back on a farm.

Days start early on the farm for Uncle Alan, even earlier for Aunt Margaret. Downstairs, the sounds and aroma of breakfast on the go would draw us slowly out of our beds. Depending on what Uncle Alan had lined up for work, we would make a decision as to whether we would go with him. If they were making hay, we would go and ride along with him on the wagon. Other times when the men were harvesting, Aunt Margaret would pack a picnic basket and we would go have our teatime out in the field with Uncle Alan. If he was ploughing the fields or spreading manure, we would stay around the farm and wait for friends to come and play.

Comic book heroes were always a constant playtime theme. Robin Hood, Ivanhoe, or Cowboys and Indians were all characters we pretended to be. Disputes were always common, quarrelling over who was going to be the hero and who should be the villains. Arguments were usually settled by making the young ones the bad men, again! There was always an outcry from the titches as to the unfairness of the situation, but with the thought of sitting on the sidelines while the rest of us played; they reluctantly took their place on the agreed side.

Although told to stay out of the hay barn, it was too much of a temptation as a place to play and build forts: hiding in the hay whenever a farmhand made an appearance. Knowing what we were up to though, I'm sure they just turned a blind eye to the whole situation. The wooden apple boxes stacked at the back of the pig barn were another great source of building material for forts too, but again, these areas were off limits to kids. There were times we would raid Aunt Margaret's vegetable patch and retreat back to our fort to feast on our ill-gotten gains. A stick of rhubarb with a hand full of sugar snuck out of the kitchen was one of my favourites.

In the evening, there was always time for a game of hide-n-seek or kick-the-can, with Uncle Alan and Aunt Margaret and a few of the village kids. At eight o'clock, it would be time to call it a day. After a quick snack, it was up the stairs and into bed. Lying there on those warm summer nights, we were lulled to sleep by the sound of music coming from a record player Aunt Margaret had acquire from her parents for her twenty-first birthday. In the morning, sunlight shone through the leaves of a giant conker tree outside our window. With fingers of light dancing across the bedroom walls, a gentle breeze drifts slowly through an open window, and the sounds of barnyard chatter coming from outside would slowly lull us awake. However, the tranquility of the morning would soon be broken by the sound of Aunt Margaret calling up the stairs "Come on, get out of that bed, else there'll be no breakfast," indicated the start of a new day.

It was Saturday. We were looking forward to a visit from our mum. She came every week for a visit, but not this time. A polio outbreak in the area had the health authority put the farm under quarantine. It was an upsetting time for my mother, as she was not aloud anywhere near the farm for two weeks. To ease her mind, Aunt Margaret wrote my mother a letter assuring her that all precaution had been made and not to worry.

At the time, I remember seeing a picture in the newspaper of a young boy crippled for life by polio and unable to breath on his own. He would have to spend the rest of his life in an iron lung, a machine that allowed him to breathe. With that picture in mind, we sat around in the hayloft unable to comprehend what life would be like in one of those machines. With kids coming down with the infection in ever-increasing numbers, there was a desperate search to locate the source of the polio. It was a very scary time of life for many children living in the area. Much to everyone's relief, later that summer, the origin of the polio was finally identified as coming from a river near Maidstone, a popular place where kids liked to swim.

With the polio quarantine over, life got back to normal on the farm. My mum resumed her Saturday visits and with it, our usual walk into Pluckley to spend our pocket money. It was a leisurely one-mile walk down to the village along a narrow country lane. A small matchbox camera in the local shop had caught my eye, and with the five-shilling allowance I purchased my first camera. Photos taken that summer I still have today, some fifty years later.

Soon days turned into weeks and the weeks slipped quickly by. After six great weeks at Pevington Farm with the Sages, the summer holidays were soon coming to an end. There was a melancholy feeling in the air that last week and for the first time, Karen and I had mixed feelings about leaving Uncle Alan and Aunt Margaret and going back to Hothfield.

Sunday, my mum and Mrs. Housdan arrived to take us home, with the promise from Uncle Alan and Aunt Margaret that we could come back again next year.

Arriving back home my mother had a surprise for my sister and me. Our brand new bikes were waiting for us. True to her word, my Raleigh bike had cable brakes with a five speed derailleur gears, the only five-speed bike in the village at the time.

With all its faults and failures, Hothfield was a great place to grow up in as a kid. One of the highlights of the year for village kids was the annual Christmas party put on by the Hothfield Women's Committee, helped along by many of the mothers. I do not think as kids, we ever realized how hard these women worked through out the year to put this party on. Funds raised by auctions, rummage sales and monthly whist drives were put towards the party. It was highly anticipated by the hundred and fifty plus children in the village, young and old alike, especially families who did not have a lot. Sandwiches, fancy cakes and biscuits all piled high on plates; along with juice, ice cream, and jellies seem to have no end. At the far-end of the hall was a large decorated Christmas tree. After saying grace, lizards like hands shot out, paying little attention to the sandwiches and going straight for the cakes, buns and biscuits to fill our bellies. After devouring all the food, there would be the mandatory singsong of a few Christmas carols. Following a game or two of Blind Man's Bluff, or Pin the Tail on the Donkey, there was a mad scramble as a shower of balloons came down from the ceiling. Once the mayhem with the balloons was over with, kids were reassembled to watch a Punch and Judy show. The highlight of the evening would be Santa Clause with his sack full of presents, one for each child, along with a bag of sweets and an orange. After the Christmas party, Hothfield children would then look forward to a special outing in the spring. This was when Mrs. Tufton would hire buses to take all the children of the village down to the seaside for the day.

There were no organized sports outside of school hours in the village. Therefore, in the evenings after tea, the village green became a central gathering place for kids to play their games and hang out. Depending on the season, it might be cricket or football for the boys or rounders for the girls. A game of football could have as many as twenty kids per side, all running in different directions, wanting to be on the winning side. The goalposts were a couple of coats strategically placed at either end of the green. No need for a referee, or boundaries, we all knew what the rules were. The older kids ruled. The boundaries were made up with the bogs on one side of the village green and School Road on the other. Therefore, as long as the ball was on the green, it was in play.

At the far end of the common was what we called the duck pond. A stick, some thread and a ball of bread-dough on the end of a bent pin would suffice for fishing gear. Other kids would grab one of their mother's old nylons, wrap it around a coat hanger and tie it onto the end of a stick to make a fishing net. Many an afternoon would be whiled away catching minnows with our inventive gear.

For my twelfth birthday, I finally got my fishing rod. The only problem with that was all the lakes and rivers around Hothfield were privately owned. To get any decent fishing, one would have to do a little poaching. That meant while out angling for a little sport, we needed to keep one eye on our rod and the other on the lookout for the local gamekeeper. There were many times, when we saw him coming; we would make a run for it. Other times, he would lay in wait for us at one of our favourite fishing holes. Catching us red-handed, he would immediately march us out to the road with the threat of confiscating all our fishing gear if he ever caught us back there again. Worst still, he would refuse to hire us for any upcoming hunting beats.

Hothfield Common never ceased to be a source of activity for many kids growing up in the village; forts built, bike trails cut and trees climbed. Many an hour would be spent perched high in the canopy of a large oak or chestnut tree. With our imagination-running wild, we visualized ourselves flying Spitfires against the mighty Luftwaffe or in a Lancaster Bomber on a "Dam Buster" mission.

Talents would sometimes turn to kite making. Dried bamboo sticks, gathered from Hothfield Lake and tied together in the shape of a cross, made up the frame. An old newspaper cut-up and folded over the bamboo frame, made up the body of the kite. Crumpled up newspaper in the shape of little bows were then tied together with string to make up the tail of the kite. After attaching a large ball of string to the bamboo frame, we were ready to launch. There was always a lot of running back and forth on the common before the kite became airborne. When it finally did take flight, there was a great deal of satisfaction as we watched our handy work sail above the treetops.

Another source of entertainment on the common was the local sewage plant. A flimsy fence surrounded the plant and was very little deterrent to kids who wanted inside to play. In one corner of the plant sat a large cement-holding tank for collecting the raw fecal matter. Over top of the holding tank was a narrow metal catwalk. Off to the other side of the field was a long four-armed pipe system that turned slowly on a central axis over a bed of cinders. This was the filtering system for dispersing of the effluent. For some kids, riding around on these pipes became a cheap merry-go-round. One day, while we were returning home from the duck pond, we passed by the sewage plant and found three young panic-stricken boys. They claimed that one of their friend's had fallen off the catwalk into the holding tank. After reporting the incident to PC Doors, we returned to the sewage plant to await the Charing Fire Brigade. Arriving at the scene, the firemen proceeded to drain the large cement-holding tank. A short time later, the dismal sight of a five-year-old boy's lifeless body was pulled from the tank on the end of a pike-pole. The young fellow was a neighbour of ours and lived just across from us in Common Way. The image of that little boy on the end of a pike-pole burned an unforgettable picture in my mind that stayed there for many months. Not long after the drowning, the council built a more substantial fence around the facility.

Other times on weekends, we would spend many hours roaming throughout country lanes, past farms, over fields and into the neighbouring villages. Little Chart had a paper mill with a pond at the back that was a good place for pike fishing. Charing always appealed to us; it had a park with swings, a slide and seesaws. A hike up the North Downs by way of West Well is were we picked up our supply of natural chalk for marking out our games on the roads at home. Walking down Pilgrim's Way for about a mile, we would then cut across country to an apple orchard at Tutt Hill for a little scrumping. At the old railway bridge, if the timing was right, you could stand on top of the bridge and be lost in a cloud of smoke and ash as a steam train passed below.

Along with the new estate, there were a few new businesses.

Mr. Foreman ran a small convenience store on the main street. This is where we bought our mother a pair of house-slippers each year for her Christmas present. Mr. Foreman also did a little barbering on the side. Mr. Sainsbury ran the local grocery shop that supplied most of the village needs. One of the things that always fascinated me at the shop was watching them cut cheese with a wire. Biscuits at that time came in large tins and were sold individually or by the dozen. Tins would have a number of broken biscuits that we bought for half price. Across from Sainsbury's, Mr. Reed ran a small green grocer's shop on the weekend. Mr. Spicer was the local butcher. Here, sides of beef, pork and lamb hung on large hooks, along with fresh chicken and rabbit, a display guaranteed to shock today's "Food Inspectors." In the center of the shop, there was a large, round, wooden stump approximately three feet in diameter. This was used to cut meat on. Every Friday afternoon, my mum would go to Mr. Spicer's and buy me a steak for my dinner. Mr. Manson was the local publican. This is where my mother would send me from time to time to pick up her favourite, milk stout, whenever she felt like celebrating some special occasion. With televisions becoming a fixture in many homes, Mr. Higgs open up a small TV and radio retail and repair shop in the village and soon TV antennas were popping up on chimneys all over the estate.

Chapter 10

Hothfield Home

*There are places I remember all my life, though
some have changed some forever, not for better.
Lennon & McCartney*

Nineteen fifty six was the last summer we would spend with Aunt Margaret and Uncle Alan at Pevington Farm, although they have remained dear friends over these many years. After two great summers with them, they were now foster parents to a baby girl. Next would come Tony and Maria, and so it went. Over the next ten years, the Sage's would raise a total of seven foster children before starting their own family.

Karen finished Hothfield Primary School that same year. Having failed her eleven plus exam along with her good friend Dawn, they both moved on to Ashford South Secondary School for Girls. The following year, I would sit the dreaded eleven plus exam myself, and fall short, along with most of the Hothfield students. We then moved on to Secondary schools in Ashford, where girls and boys were educated in separate schools. There was a general feeling among parents who had children in small rural schools that their children were taught very little in preparation for the eleven plus exam. Therefore, it was a fait accompli that most of them would fail. Three students from Little Chart who went to Hothfield Primary did pass the eleven plus that year, as their parents were able to afford tutors for them. They now moved on to Grammar School.

Moving from a small rural primary school in Hothfield to a large secondary school in Ashford came as a bit of a shock for most of us. Apart from the pecking order in the schoolyard and the intimidation by the older boys, there were always prefects wandering the playgrounds and hallways looking for any violation of the school rules. This gave them an excuse to haul you up before the headmaster, thereby justifying their position. The school day at Ashford South started with a full assembly in the gym. After a couple of songs from the hymnal and the announcements, it would be time to get working for the day.

The switch from pencils used in primary school, to ink pens in secondary school was another awkward adjustment. At the time, teachers at Ashford South did not allow ballpoint pens. If you could not afford a fountain pen, the school would issue you the standard dip-pen and inkwell. The system took a little getting use to and with ink spills and splashes all over my notebooks that first year; I went through copious amounts of blotting paper.

School went well for me that first year at Ashford South, with the exception of one small incident. My mother always did her best to make sure Karen and I were neat and tidy for school each day. In our early teen years, boys tended to have an aversion to haircuts, myself included. One morning while in class, Mr. Llewellyn, my homeroom teacher decided to make me the object of a little classroom ridicule. "Roders," he said, "I don't know whether to give you two-n-six *(two shilling and six pence)* for a haircut or buy you a violin." I did not take it too personally. It was confirmation that I did indeed have the longest hair in the class. This gave me bragging rights among my peers. However, when I went home and told my mother, she felt quite insulted. The next day she was down the school to have a little chat with Mr. Llewellyn. Telling him in no uncertain terms, to mind his own business when it came to John's personal grooming. This did not sit well with him and for the rest of that year he never failed to take a dig at me any chance he got. At the end of that school year following final exams, it was determined that I had finished top of my form. A standing that should have put me in line for a book-prize on awards day. Mr. Llewellyn, however, in his biased sense of fairness, found another boy he thought more worthy.

Teachers at Ashford South had their preferred forms of punishment too when dealing with a student he considered unruly. A good rap on the back of the knuckles with a yardstick was one teacher's preferred choice of punishment. "Little Ernie," the art instructor, his favourite form of laying on the agony was a leather strap across your hand. Some kids in anticipation of the slap from the strap would draw their hand away, much to the annoyance of Mr. Marcroft, who had put a great deal of energy into his swing to maximize the sting. In doing so, the student would now have to endure two slaps of the strap. He was always careful not to thwack you on your drawing hand, thereby giving you no excuse not to finish your artwork. The gym teacher had a size thirteen plimsoll with a hard rubber sole. This would leave a large welt on your backside in the shape of the shoe. The music teacher, Mrs. Solly, God bless her, probably had the toughest job in the whole school. She had the task of teaching a bunch of unrefined teenage boys how to sing, "Green Grow the Rushes O," or play "Scarborough Fair," on the recorder. All we wanted to do at the time was get a guitar and sing "Blue Suede Shoes."

From time to time, Mr. Watts, the headmaster, would monitor the hallways. With a cane hooked over his shoulder and concealed under his jacket, he would be on the lookout for any minor breach of school rules. Students caught sliding down banisters, running up or down stairs two at a time or performing any kind of tomfoolery in the halls, he would take the cane out from under his jacket and give the student a couple of good cracks on the hand, careful not to hit you on your writing hand.

For major violations of school rules, such as back-chatting teachers, fighting with prefects, offensive language, or any other violation deemed major by Mr. Watts, he would call for a full assembly after lunch. Students who were responsible for breaking these school rules would be marched into the gym and up onto the stage. After the headmaster had lectured the student body on the disobedience of said individuals, he would then cane the offenders in front of the entire school assembly. Confident the public flogging would discourage any more such misbehaviour by other students in the future. Standard outlay would generally be six of the best applied to the student's rear-end. The headmaster, in his fervour to get his message across, would come down hard on the boy in an attempt to get him to cry-out in pain. After one of these thrashing, a student was unable to sit down comfortably for a few hours and was left bruised and marked for days.

In the sixties, there was a move to do away with corporal punishment in schools. In due course, some students started to take matters into their own hands. The last time I ever saw a student caned at school was when the headmaster came to our homeroom one afternoon to discipline a boy. He had apparently been in a bit of a punch-up with another boy. The headmaster called him up to the front of the class, bent him over a desk and in a determined manner, proceeded to strike him repeatedly on the backside. After the third or forth wallop, the boy had had enough. In a determined move and to the shock of the entire class and the headmaster, the boy jumped up, turned around and grabbed the cane out of the headmaster's hand and threw it against the far wall, and ran out of the room. This sent a message to the students that they did not have to put up with this kind of brutality anymore.

After spending the day cooped-up in school, under strict rules and corporal punishment for the slightest infraction, boys had a tendency to let loose a little, once they were beyond the school limits. Wednesday was market day. On the way uptown in the afternoon to catch the bus home, we would always make a detour through the marketplace. Here, we took great pleasure in tossing the discarded rotten fruit left behind in the stalls at any other kids who took up the challenge. Management at the market complained to the school, as they did not like the mess left behind or the clean up. One of the supervisors at the market was Hooky; the nickname given to him as he had lost one of his hands and in its place, he had a metal hook. He was the one man in the market who could really put the fear of God into us. When he chased us, we would run like crazy, as we never knew what he might do to us with that hook, if he ever caught us. Uptown, store windows were not off limits to the odd piece of misguided fruit either. Again, school uniforms usually identified students and the headmaster dealt with them the next day. A few more kids took great pleasure in blitzing the Woolworth store after school, with the idea of doing a little pilfering. Afterwards, they would show up back at the bus stop trying to impress the younger students with their ill-gotten gains. One day, two Hothfield boys were caught red-handed by the store manager. They ended up in the backseat of a "Black Mariah," for a ride home to their parents.

With no designated school buses at the time, students traveled on public transport along with everybody else. With the newfound freedom that came from riding the bus to and from Ashford each day, attitudes and egos of some boys tended to get a little puffed up and out of control as the school years went by. The bus that came through Hothfield in the morning was a double-decker and boys liked to take over the upstairs. As the bus entered the village, it needed to slow down at a corner just before it got to the bus stop. Waiting at that corner, we would jump onto the open platform at the back of the bus, and make our way upstairs. Securing seats on the upper deck, we were free to heckle out of the top windows at passers-by without too much consequence. This did not sit well with the bus drivers or conductors. They felt that the pushing and shoving to jump onto the back of a moving bus would eventually end in a serious injury. The practice finally came to a stop when the bus conductors started taking names of the offenders off their bus passes. Identified by their school uniforms, they would face disciplinary action by the headmaster when they got to school. The most disliked of all the bus conductors was a fellow nicknamed Scrooge. He always had a moan-on and put up with very little nonsense. From time to time, he would show up on the afternoon bus run. Standing on the platform below, kids would "Take the Mick," by shouting insults down at him from the upper deck. Scrambling up the stairs, he would threaten to put the perpetrator of the nasty comments off the bus if ever he caught them. One day, following an exchange with a boy, he stopped the bus and refused to go again until the student got off. In solidarity with one of our mates, three of us got off the bus and enjoyed a leisurely walk home.

The final straw for the Hothfield students riding on public transport came one morning on the upper deck of the bus. A shoving match broke out between two boys, one who wanted to get off the bus when it came to a stop uptown, the other boy told him to sit back down. As he tried to shuffle past a couple of other kids seated beside him, he was pushed backwards. Tripping over feet as he fell, his rear-end smashed out the bus window. As chance would have it, the falling glass narrowly missed one of our schoolmasters as he rode passed the bus on his bike. The replacement of that window would cost the four students sitting in that seat a total of two pounds. My mother was not pleased with me when she got my portion of the bill in the mail. Ten shillings was a half-day's pay for her at that time.

The School Board, Transit Company, Ashford Market and a number of other businesses wanted something done about the "Hothfield ilk." Their attitudes and behaviour were inexcusable both on and off the buses. The answer would finally come in the form of a private bus. There would be no more Hothfield students riding on public transport during school hours, or running roughshod through the town. The bus would come from Ashford in the morning, pick up only Hothfield students, and deliver them right to the front gates of the Ashford South Secondary School. The same thing would happen in the afternoon. The bus would park right outside the school gate and take students directly back home to Hothfield. On the cold, rainy days of winter, when many students faced a one-mile bone chilling walk up-town to catch their buses home. Students from Hothfield came out of the school and stepped aboard a nice warm bus, taunting fellow students out of the windows as we drove by them on our way home.

With summer coming on, Karen and I knew we would not be going back to Pevington Farm. Instead, we would look for ways to earn some money on our summer holidays. Mr. Coles always needed some hoeing done and there was always fruit to pick throughout the summer. From time to time, Sir Reginald Roots would have a hunting beat. He paid kids fifteen shillings for the day, plus a large bottle of Tizer. The men got a pound plus beer, not a bad day's pay for a walk in the woods. The fifth of November was Guy Fawks day. Leading up to that night, Hothfield kids would build a large bonfire on the common. We would then make an effigy of Guy Fawks, put him in a wheelbarrow and wheel him around the village chanting, "Remember, remember, the fifth of November," and in the process, we would cadge a few pennies to buy fireworks. On Guy Fawks night, the dummy would be place on top of the bonfire and burned. Parents sat on the wall along School Road to watch the festivities, while keeping an eye on the younger children. When the bonfire finally burned down and the last of the fireworks had fizzled, it would be time to bake potatoes and chestnuts in the hot coals. A little carol singing door to door in the neighbourhood at Christmas time would also add a few pennies to the party coffers. One of the landowners living in Hothfield and well known for her generosity was Mrs. Tufton. Although she lived a half mile up a dark lane, she made it worth the walk to go sing her a few carols. I remember one Christmas when Tufton's farm had raised turkeys and were paying a half-crown for every bird you killed and plucked. This was very good money at the time. Hunting rabbits was always a bit of sport, good exercise and the source of a little pocket money too, with the sale of a rabbit or two. We would spend many hours on the common digging them out. One day, much to our relief, David Neaves, a friend of mine got his dad to buy him a ferret. This made the pursuit of dinner a whole lot easier. A good dog could pick up the scent of a rabbit down the hole. Having detected a rabbit, we would cover all the surrounding pop holes with nets; then send the ferret into the burrow. The rabbit, threatened by the presence of the ferret, would make its escape by way of one of the pop holes. Entangled in the net, it would thus meet its demise. There was always a bit of a balancing act with ferrets. If you fed them too much before you went out, there was a good chance they would fall asleep down the rabbit hole. On the other hand, if you did not give them something to eat they might catch the rabbit, have a feed and still fall asleep down the hole. There were many times we sat for hours waiting on the ferret to come out of the burrow.

With the overabundance of rabbits in England at the time and a glut of them living on the common, the destruction of crops was costing farmers millions of pounds each year. Apart from hunting them, farmers from around Hothfield spent time on the common one summer gassing their burrows. This only slowed the population down for a while. Myxomatosis, by all accounts, was launched illegally in France in the early fifties to control the rabbit population on a private estate. It's debatable whether its introduction into England was intentional or by accident. The virus had a debilitating effect on rabbits, causing tumours on the skin, swollen heads and bugged out eyes. In the later stages, rabbits blinded by the illness would hop helplessly into neighbourhoods, and lie dying a slow and agonizing death on many streets. A situation deplored by many people at the time as inhumane and cruel. About that same time, city dwellers from London and surrounding area who found the cost of living in the urban centers more and more prohibitive began to move out to the country, preferring to commute to the city for work. Along with them came some of their city ideals. Fox hunting would be high on their list of priorities as a country way of life they would need to put a stop to. Next would be chickens kept in backyards. Roasters, apparently, woke them up too early on a Saturday morning after they had spent a late Friday night up in London, clubbing after work. Slow moving tractors and the mud they left on the roads also became an irritant to these transplanted urbanites.

Myxomatosis, however, did put an end to our rabbit hunting adventures and a source of a little pocket money. On the other hand, in the process of digging out rabbits we regularly came across old army surplus buried on the common after the war. With the loss of the rabbit hunting, we now turned our attention to looking for more of this World War II booty.

While at school in post war England, teachers warned students many times to report any suspicious looking munitions they might find lying around. For a couple of my mates and me, that message went unheeded one day when we found an old mortar shell. With the bomb in hand, we took turns throwing it at trees to see if it would explode. Luckily it never did. When one of our friends went home, he told his dad about what we had been up to, his dad went ballistic. Mr. Sharman, our friends' dad, insisted we take him down to Hothfield Lake, where the bomb was; there he threw it as far as he could into the lake. On the way back home, he gave us all a good talking to, as did PC Doors, the local police officer, when he found out.

Despite the warnings, we still spent our weekends digging up the army surplus: canteen boxes filled with enamel plates and cups, brass shell casings, metal helmets and old gas masks. Then one day, much to our surprise, the mother load. Live bullets! These were leftovers from the war and buried on the common, either by the Americans troops who were stationed at Pluckley, or the Reemee, an army depot just outside of Ashford. After removing the gunpowder from the casing, we replaced the head, polished up the bullets and they became a hot swapping item. Taking the ammo to school one day, we traded them off for cash and treats from the Tuck Shop. The next morning at school, while waiting for class to begin and in the middle of some more bullet business, a police car pulled into the schoolyard. Five minutes later, three Hothfield lads found themselves in the headmaster's office. The father of one of the students we had done a swap with the day before, had concerns about bullets at the school and reported it to the police. After a twenty-minute interrogation by the police as to how we had come to be in possession of the live bullets, it was determined that there would be no more digging up army surplus on Hothfield Common. All agreed that there would be no more bullets at school either.

Right up until the late fifties, the Reemee in Ashford were still using Hothfield Common extensively for their army manoeuvres. To pass the time on weekends, we would run all over the common, following the soldiers and watching them from a safe distance as they went through their military exercises. One day, while they were going through some training routines and throwing smoke bombs around, I noticed that one of the smoke canisters did not detonate. After the army had finished its drills for the day and left, we went into action looking for our next little adventure. After a few minutes of searching, I found the smoke bomb lying in a thicket of heather. John Bull, one of the fellows with us, had a brother David, who had completed his two-year stint in the British army. Taking it back to his house, we thought his brother might have had some experience with such devices. However, David was not at home at the time, so we took the canister into the backyard and did a little tinkering with it ourselves. Smoke bombs, thankfully, do not explode. They just pop open and dispense plumbs of smoke, in this particular case, extremely thick blue smoke. With the cloud of smoke now choking the neighbourhood, it caused quite a panic with a number of women who had their Sunday washing out on the line. Mrs. Murrell, whose garden backed onto Bull's backyard, had a line full of clean white sheets drying. She was not happy with us as she came running out to salvage her laundry. Mr. Doors, the well-regarded member of the Hothfield constabulary, had a report that a smoke bomb had gone off in the village and was not pleased. By now, PC Doors had had enough of bullets, bombs and mortars in the village and was not going to put up with it any longer. Any more reports of munitions that were likely to explode and injure people, and he would be handing out court summonses.

Steve Mathews was a good friend of mine, his dad had a pulp logging business and during the summer holidays, I would work for him. For thirty shillings a week, we would pack pulp logs out of the woods, load them onto the lorry, and take them to the mill. Saturday mornings I did meat delivery for Mr. Spicer, the local butcher, for which he paid me ten shillings. This gave me a total of two pounds in my pocket at the end of each week. Saturday afternoons, after delivering links of sausage, joints of lamb, roasts of beef and pork chops to the women of the village for their Sunday dinner, it would be time to go to town and have a little fun. Donning my Italian pin stripe suit, *(tailor made at Burtons, thanks to mum)* bootlace tie, winkle-picker shoes, and a coiffeur a'la Elvis Presley, we were off to the pictures. If we were lucky, Steve's dad would be going into town and we would hop on the back of the lorry for a ride.

There were two picture houses in Ashford: the Odeon and the Cinema. The Odeon carried the more Hollywood-type pictures, with Doris Day, Grace Kelly, and Rock Hudson. The Cinema was apt to show the more risqué European pictures with Gina Lola or Brigitte Bardot. At that time in our lives, a glimpse of Bardot boobs, or Gina's long lacy legs, usually trumped Day or Kelly's pretty face or Rock Hudson's good looks. As we were only fourteen at the time, and most of these European pictures were restricted, we needed to look a little more grown-up. A pack of cigarettes would usually do the trick. Not the cheap Weights or Woodbines either. No, we were out to impress. It was Rothmans filter tips all the way. Lighting up in the lobby, we would stroll up to the ticket window doing our best impression of James Dean; cigarette dangling off the bottom lip. Giving the ticket attendant a devious smile, and taking a long drag on the fag, we would splash down a pound note for the tickets. It worked most of the time.

There was no specific start time for a film in those days. Theatres usually opened in the early afternoon, ran a newsreel, sometimes a cartoon then a "B" rated movie before the main feature. This format would run consecutively throughout the day until ten in the evening, keeping us entertained until the doors closed.

In the summer of fifty-seven, my mother received a letter from her sister Nell in Canada. The letter came as a bit of a surprise. It had been more than ten years since the fiasco with Reg and Nora over the market garden and the three of them had immigrated to Canada. Nell had married a Canadian shortly after arriving in Canada. They had four girls, Ann, Verna, Carol and Kip, and living in Nelson, British Columbia. Over the course of the next year, she kept up a friendly correspondence with my mother. In one of her letters, she asked my mother if she had ever considered immigrating to Canada. Running the idea past my sister and me, she found very little support from Karen, but my mother and I were both in favour of the move. Being a single parent with two dependants and no profession, my mother thought there would be few prospects for her being considered as a candidate for immigration. However, she did make some tentative enquiries to Canada House and received a letter back suggesting that there might be a possibility of immigration. She would need to get a letter from her sister and her husband in Canada to vouch for us, saying that we would not be a burden on the country for five years. They would also need to provide us with a place to live as well. If any Canadian laws were broken within that five-year period, we could face deportation.

One month later, a letter from Bill and Nell came in the mail confirming that they would indeed vouch for us. They also mentioned that there was a two-bedroom suite in the basement of their house for us to live in. My mother, with letter in hand, now made an appointment at Canada House to set up an interview. Upon our first visit to Canada House, the staff set the paper work in motion. The Canadian authorities would need to interview Bill and Nell and do an inspection of their home to confirm that all was up to par.

My mother's next step was to set in motion applications for passports. She was having trouble tracking down a birth certificate for me. Born at home in my grandparent's home in Holland just after the war, she feared that my birth might not have been registered. She only had a baptismal certificate from the Seamen's Church in Noordzingel. My mother was also in for a surprise of her own. She had gone up to Somerset House in London for what should have been a routine check on her birth records and pick up her certificate. After spending the morning searching birth records, she had not been successful. She had found all her siblings, but not her own name and date. Taking a break for lunch, she returned in the afternoon for another go. After a couple more hours of unsuccessful searching, she reported to one of the staff, convinced that her birth date may not have been registered. He assured my mother that if she were born in England, it would be in their files. He told her with a name like Regan, there was a good possibility it might have been misspelled. She should go back and check on some variation of the spelling. With that in mind, she went back and started looking through the list of Reagen's. Within a half-hour, she found it, Matilda Maud Reagen, born December 27th 1909, Marcus Street, Plaistow, London. Her last name had been misspelled. Under her breath, she had a few choice words for her father.

With application forms for British passports filled out and in the mail, my mother did have one small concern on my application. She was still unable to track down a birth certificate for me. She had a bigger concern a few weeks later when my application for a British passport came back. The enclosed letter stated that the applicant, Simon John James Roders, born in Holland of a Dutch father, was in fact Dutch by nationality, not English. My mother now had to apply to the Dutch Consul in London for a passport for me. Meantime, there was still a desperate search going on for my birth certificate.

My mother's next task was to check out fares for our passage to Canada. As it turned out, going by ship from Southampton to Montreal and then taking a train from Montreal to Nelson B.C. would be the most economical. Even so, my mother figured out that at her current rate of pay, it would take her five years to save the fare. To speed things up, she took a part time afternoon job at *Smiths Crisps* in Ashford in order to save more money. This meant that she would finish work at four-thirty at Hothfield Hospital, hop a bus into Ashford and do a four-hour shift at *Smiths*, coming home at eleven o'clock at night. Karen, who was still not in favour of the move, made it known among her friends that her mother would neither keep up the pace nor get the fare together. Just the kind of challenge my mother needed to hear. She had also just purchased our first TV set on the Never Never. The TV went back in order to save more money. After two years at *Smith Crisps*, my mother had saved up enough money for our boat and train fare.

In the meantime, Canada House had written my mother, informing her that the living conditions at Nell and Bill's did not meet Canadian immigration standards. Until they made changes to the home, Canadian authorities would not give the go ahead for a move. My mother wrote a letter to Nell informing her of the letter she had received from Canada House. Nell in turn wrote back telling my mother she was aware of immigrations concerns and that they were addressing the problem.

Canadian immigration also needed to see a copy of my mother's divorce papers and confirmation that she had custody of her children; she had neither of these. My mother had not seen Simon since that fateful night at the in-laws flat in Rotterdam some twelve years ago and did not relish the thought of seeing him again. Getting in touch with a solicitor, he assured my mother that a face-to-face meeting would not be necessary; he would set in motion the required paper work to secure a divorce and custody of her children. My father had no opposition to the divorce, but he did object to Karen and me going to live in Canada. He was under the impression that we were going to stay with Reg and Nora. My father was still holding a grudge against them after they had skipped the country and left him holding the bag regarding the market garden. However, he did finally relent, when he knew we were going to live with Aunt Nell.

With the divorce now finalized and custody of the children settled, my mother focused her attention on my passport. With only a few months left before we set sail for Canada, my birth certificate had still not been located. The Dutch Consul would not issue a passport until it was found. Finally, with only a few weeks left before our sailing date my mother made a personal trip to the Dutch Consulate in London. Here she appealed for some resolution to my passport dilemma. I'm not sure what strings were pulled or buttons pushed, but she walked out of the Dutch Consulate at the end of that day with my passport in hand

With the sale of our entire home furnishing, my mother received only pittance of what it was worth. This left us short of spending money for the voyage. Leaving Hothfield that day, we made our way over to Aunt Rose. John Ward, David Marsh and Dawn Grant, close friends of my sister, came along to wish us well. At Aunt Rose and Uncle Barry's place that night, we had our farewell shindig. On the morning of May 3rd 1961, we caught the train down to Southampton, boarded the Cunard ship *"Saxonia,"* and sailed off to Canada

In many ways, Hothfield will always be home to us. We spent many of the happiest days of our life growing up there. It was the first place my mother managed to get on her feet and establish the kind of life she had always intended for her family. A loving mother who had stood tall in the midst of much adversity, her hard work and dedication to our well-being was always her main concern. Not one for letting the grass grow under her feet though, my mother saw Canada as her next step in the progression of making a better life for us.

John Roders was born in Rotterdam Holland, to an English mother and a Dutch father. After a turbulent three-year marriage, his mother left Holland and moved back to England. He recounts, along with his mother, her early years growing up in London between two world wars, and of living with his sister Karen and his mum during the aftermath of World War II in Kent. John tells how his mum survived as a single parent. He tells her story by recreating the drama, anxiety, sadness and yes, humour too, as Tilly struggled to maintain a safe and happy family environment for John and his sister.

John now lives in Terrace, British Columbia, Canada where he has worked as a hairstylist for the past forty years. He is married to Ruth, his wife of 30 years. They have two grown-up sons, Timothy and Steven.